The Rest of the Week

The Rest of the Week

Fr. Kenneth J. Roberts

PAX TAPES, INC.
Florissant, MO 63031

DEDICATION

To the many thousands of wonderful men,
some of whom I know — most of whom I
don't; many of whom are extraordinary — most
of whom are not. They are white, black, red,
yellow. . . . They are in every field of endeavor,
in every corner of the earth. . . . They are
saints and sinners — the greatest international
brotherhood the world has ever known . . .
my brother priests.

FOREWORD

He is praised, criticized, acclaimed, ridiculed, respected, insult-
ed, accepted, questioned, appreciated and misunderstood. He is
granted such privileges as preferred service in a restaurant,
sales tax exemptions, attention at parties, the good china when
dining in a private home . . . and discounts! His obligations con-
sist of visiting the sick, burying the dead, keeping late hours
whenever necessary, making himself available at all times,
keeping sometimes painful confidences, spending long hours
counseling, being present at many, many meetings and social
gatherings, forfeiting the right to love a woman and father children, and *always*, always being aware he is a representative of
the greatest fraternity in the world . . . the priesthood! What
qualifications must a man have to become a part of this fraternity? He must be of sound moral character, average intelligence,
and most of all, he must have a desire to continue the work of
Christ through the Church. Do these things make him different
from other men? Does he feel what they feel? Think how they
think? Have the same frustrations? Have the same needs?
Temptations? Worries? Anxieties?

In the past decade, perhaps more than in any other era, the
image of the priesthood has changed . . . sometimes to the confusion of the laity. The Bing Crosby-Barry Fitzgerald characters
busied themselves with meeting the parish mortgage and en-
couraging youngsters to go "Swinging on a Star." Now the media

have introduced us to a new breed of priests — some involved in drug rehabilitation, anti-war demonstrations, social injustices and even politicking. These priests, who belong to the minority, are good copy. Because of their unique apostolates, they are granted press interviews, space in the local newspaper (along with photos), an occasional spot on a TV talk show and once in a while, time on the evening news.

The priests of the silent majority, on the other hand, are never heard from except by their parishioners on Sundays. They are not heralded, but their efforts are nonetheless exacting . . . and oftentimes, they are misunderstood. Daily each one of these priests thrashes through his own human nature in hopes that he may bring Christ to the people he serves. Always he is amazed that somehow in spite of his weaknesses, Christ gets the job done.

In this book, I have taken true experiences of a composite of priests including myself, being cautious not to betray any confidences placed in us by those we serve. All these experiences have not happened to one particular priest, but they could have; or at one particular time, but they could have; or in one given parish, but they could have. They could have happened to the priest you saw at last week's football game, the priest in the next parish, the priest that taught you, the priest that married you. They could even have happened to your parish priest!

What do I hope to accomplish? Maybe it will give the reader some insight, perhaps a better understanding of the priest in today's world . . . maybe even a little appreciation for the guy you see only on Sunday.

I don't believe there is a priest who has not been told, "You guys got it made!!!" To all of you who have made that statement and to all of you who are curious about our life-style, let's live it together. Let's go past the last Mass on Sunday. Let's live *the rest of the week.*

Kenneth J. Roberts

CONTENTS

CHAPTER 1

FRUSTRATION

(Sunday)

(Two in the afternoon and here I lie, counting venetian-blind slats . . . just as I did as a kid. I'd start from the bottom and work my way up. Funny how your eyes play tricks on you, how the lines run together and you lose your count . . . funnier, that at thirty-five, I still find it a challenge not to lose my place as I start from the bottom, up. Of course these blinds are more of a challenge than the ones that hung in my boyhood room. The ones in my old room probably weren't over two feet in length; but these are almost five feet long. And here I am on my bed counting slats and waiting for my alarm to ring. Why? Why can't I just reach over and press the button before I have to listen to that horrible ring? It's a simple matter of will power. If I turn off the alarm now, I'll lie here a little longer . . . maybe even forget that I only have half an hour for a nap; but if the ring starts, it will demand that I get up. It will take me away from my bedroom and my venetian blinds and bring me back to reality and what the rest of the day holds in store.

    (There it goes! "Old faithful" . . . right on the dot. This clock is like an old friend. How long has it been now — ten years? Ten years and it has served me well, never failed me once.) Joe reached for the alarm, silenced it and lay back on the bed again. *(Strange, I was more alert when I was counting my blinds, but as soon as I hear that ring, I get drowsy again . . . I rebel. Maybe I'm conditioned to reacting as soon as I hear that piercing sound;*

*even though I rebel against it, I do get up. Maybe I've condi-
tioned myself to react to everything almost unconsciously in the
past ten years of my life . . . but then I was well-trained. Only
last night at the cocktail party when the hostess offered me the
hors d'oeuvres tray and gave me that certain look. I saw it, I
knew what it meant, but I said "Thank you," and politely turned
my eyes to the gentlemen across from me as if I hadn't noticed
the "eye" at all. That was the proper reaction, and as always I
reacted properly. Just once I'd like to. . . . Oh well, I've traded
my counting for daydreaming now. It's two o'clock. It's Sunday.
And I have things to do.)*

Joe jumped from the bed, stretched, yawned, then grabbed
the bathrobe. *(Why didn't I go to bed at a decent hour last night
instead of getting involved in that civil-rights discussion? I
should know better. I didn't accomplish anything except making
it ten times harder to get up this morning. It's hot and humid
and I'm clammy. A shower will revive me!)*

Joe seemed to take more showers than most men. It was a
kind of sublimation for him. He felt free in the shower. As the
water cleansed his body, he felt that it also cleansed his mind.
Sometimes he felt his mind needed the shower more. How many
problems, anxieties and conflicting thoughts were stored there!

Joe whistled softly as he lathered himself, letting the warm
spray fall on his black curly hair and down his face. At thirty-
five, Joe barely looked thirty. He was a handsome man, well
over six feet tall, darkskinned with pale blue eyes. In spite of his
well-built masculine frame, many would wonder if he were a
real man, for most people with whom he came in contact never
thought of him as a man at all.

He was about to step from the shower when the housekeeper began to pound on his bedroom door. "Father Joe! Father Joe!
Can you hear me? There's a phone call for you. They said it was
very important."

"I'll take it, Mrs. Quinlan," Joe shouted as he reached for his
robe and threw a towel around his neck. Joe left wet footprints
and a trail of water as he made his way to the hall telephone outside his room.

"Father Newman speaking," he said, a little breathless as he vigorously rubbed his wet head and face with the towel.

"Joe, it's me. Did I take you away from anything?" asked Ed Pieri. Joe and Ed had been lifelong friends from grade school and seminary, right through to ordination.

"It's you! Dearie said it was important and I interrupted a shower to come to the phone. I thought it was some kind of an emergency or something."

"Not exactly, but I wanted to tell you myself. I'm leaving, Joe."

"You've been transferred?"

"No, I'm leaving the priesthood. I've had it and I'm getting out!"

"What?" Joe practically screamed into the phone. "You're out of your mind! What are you talking about?"

"Look, Joe, I only called you to tell you before you heard it from somebody else. But I've made up my mind and I'm going to talk to the 'old man,' then make an appointment with the bishop."

"For God's sake, Ed. I know you don't get along with the old man, but that's no reason to leave. Why don't you —"

"Joe," Ed interrupted, "it's no use. I've made up my mind. It's not just the fact that I don't see eye to eye with my pastor . . . it's everything." There was a short pause on the other end of the line before Ed continued, "I can't talk anymore; the boss just walked in. He's probably waiting for me again. I have to go . . ."

"Wait a second," Joe shouted. "I'll meet you tonight and we can talk."

"No use, Joe. I can't meet you tonight anyway. I have to go to that interdenominational meeting to resign my post as chairman."

"Where is it this month? I'll meet you there."

"St. Andrew's Methodist Church on Grant Street. I have to go. The old man wants to see me. I wonder what it is this time," Ed said disgustedly. "I'll see you later, Joe."

"Hold on! Did you say *Grant* or *Grand* Street? Ed? . . . Ed? . . . You still there?" Joe shouted. He was so shocked he was unaware of the water still dripping from his legs. He stood there for a moment holding the phone when Mrs. Quinlan called down

13

the hall. "Father Joe, your appointment is here. I put them in the front parlor."

"Tell them I'll be right there," Joe answered. He hung up the phone and rushed into his room to dress. *(That parlor call would be early. Why does Ed have to be such a stubborn character? What a thing to do. Call me out of the blue and tell me he's leaving. What's with him? I wish I didn't have this appointment. I could head over there right now. Couldn't do that anyway. I've got baptisms at three. If George were around I could ask him to take them for me. Monsignor Flannagan can't . . . too sick. Maybe I could ask Father Benetti. No, I'd better not . . . it would make him too nervous. There's four scheduled and if one of them starts bawling, he would get all shook. Boy, George sure cleared out of here fast after the last Mass. Come to think of it . . . I haven't seen much of that guy in weeks. He's out of the rectory more than in it. Wonder what he does with all his time . . .)*

Within minutes Joe emerged from his room again. He had to reach Ed to make sure where the meeting was. Quickly, he dialed Ascension Rectory, praying silently that Ed would answer the phone.

Mrs. Burke, the impatient housekeeper, answered. She had been at Ascension as long as the pastor, over twenty years, and had seen many assistants come and go; many believed she was instrumental in more than one departure. "Ascension!" she bellowed.

"May I talk to Father Pieri, please?"

"No, he's just left," she answered abruptly.

Joe asked if Ed had left a number where he could be reached, but the housekeeper gave a simple reply. *"No!"* and hung up the phone rudely. *(To think she was once married. Mr. Burke must have been a masochist or perhaps a saint to put up with her. It was good that the Lord gave him a merciful release and called him early in life to his heavenly reward.)*

"I don't envy you this one," Mrs. Quinlan said as she passed Joe in the hall. "Wait till you hear the commotion coming from that front parlor."

The door of the parlor was shut but Joe could still hear the voices coming from within. "For God's sake, Pam, will you sit up straight and wipe that disgusted look from your face? I know you don't have any respect for me and your father, but at least show a little courtesy to Father Newman."

"How can she? She doesn't even respect herself. If she did, she wouldn't be in this predicament . . . and neither would we!" bawled the father.

"You both kill me, you really do. Hurry up, run to the priest and tell him all your troubles. I didn't ask for your help, or his either," came the young voice sarcastically.

Joe took a deep breath as he opened the door. Mr. and Mrs. Davis rose when he entered. Pam remained slouched in her chair; she didn't even look up.

"Good afternoon, Father," greeted the couple.

"Good afternoon," Joe said as he pulled the chair from the desk and sat down. "Now, what can I do for you?"

"I'm too ashamed to tell you, Father," began Mrs. Davis, "and to think what we've done for that girl. Everything . . . the best education, clothes. Our home was always open to her friends. She has never wanted for a thing. We always taught her right from wrong, ever since she was a little girl . . . and now this." Mrs. Davis started sobbing.

"What my wife is trying to say, Father, is that we just can't understand why Pam could have put herself in this position. As my wife said, Pam has always come first —"

"What they're both trying to tell you is, I'm pregnant!" interrupted the girl. She was looking at Joe with contempt. Suddenly she swung her head toward her parents. "Now that wasn't so hard, was it? Why can't you just say it? *Pam is pregnant!*"

"Don't be rude, Pam," scolded the mother, then she began to cry again. "After all we've tried to do for that girl. She always came first in our lives . . . always."

"Always, my foot! Always when you both weren't too busy impressing your square friends." Pam was screaming; she began to mimic her parents in an exaggeratingly mock sophisticated tone. "See my house! See my car! See my pool! See my Pam! See Pam run! See Pam smile! See Pam play! See my Pam! But you know what, Mother? You never saw me at all! Neither one of you ever saw *me!* I have to agree with one thing though, you gave me everything . . . everything money could buy!" Pam slouched deeper in her chair.

"That's enough!" Mr. Davis said, half-rising from his seat.

"What's wrong, Pops? Did I hit home?" Pam said sarcastically.

"Pam, please! We came here to ask Father Newman's advice," the mother broke in.

"I don't want his advice. I told you I know what I'm doing. I can take care of myself. Jack wants me and the baby. I'm not asking for your advice, money, blessings . . . *nothing!* I just want you to leave me alone. Can't you understand that?" Pam was screaming again.

Joe felt as if he were a spectator at a tennis match. His head began to ache and he felt a sinking feeling in his stomach. He wanted to scream too. "How old are you, Pam?"

"Seventeen."

"Do you think you're ready for marriage?"

"Who said anything about marriage? I have no intentions of getting married," she answered defiantly. "Does that shock you?" Pam was trying hard to be offensive.

"Did you hear that?" yelled her father.

Joe nodded. "All of you had better calm down a little before we can discuss this rationally." He paused a while to let the trio collect themselves. "Do you want this baby?" Joe pivoted in his chair to face Pam. *(Smart kid . . . she could use a crack in the mouth.)*

"I wasn't exactly planning on getting pregnant, you know."

"Do you love this guy, Jack?"

"Jack is great. We really make it together and he wants me to move in right away. He said he'd take care of me. We have plenty of time to decide what to do."

"Plenty of time! Did you hear that? She's almost three months gone and she says she 'has plenty of time.' Tell me, Pam, did you and your hippie friend ever discuss giving this baby a name, or is that too old-fashioned?" Mr. Davis screamed, then threw his arms in the air in disgust.

"Had you two discussed any plans in regards to Pam's pregnancy?" Joe said, turning to the parents.

16

"We don't know what to do, Father. That's why we came to you. My wife and I are beside ourselves," answered the father.

"I'll tell you what you're *not* going to do. You're not going to shut me up in some home for unwed mothers for the next six months and tell all your dumb friends that bull that I'm away at school. I won't go!" Pam yelled, sat up in her chair and leaned forward toward her parents. "And I know you're not about to let 'little Pammy' stick around the house for the next six months so your important friends can whisper about me. Right? You don't want that, do you?"

For the next forty-five minutes Joe talked with the family, first with Pam alone, then the parents. When he brought them all together again, they all agreed to consult a Catholic Charities priest-psychologist whom Joe had recommended. At least Joe was content that he had changed the attitude of the parents somewhat, and the fact that Pam had agreed to consult another priest in the matter was a good sign too. Joe had learned in his short conversation with Pam that she hadn't been to Mass in nearly a year. She turned him off when he even began to discuss the sacraments. The parents agreed to spend some time with their daughter and try to reconstruct some of the relationship that had been lost. Another good sign.

On his way to the church to prepare for the four baptisms, Dearie stopped Joe at the door. "Mrs. Ferris is on the phone. Said she wants to talk to the Monsignor, or somebody in charge. Sounds angry, Father. Monsignor Flannagan asked not to be disturbed since he was up all night with his sick stomach again. Do you want to take it?"

"That's all I need . . . to listen to another of Mrs. Ferris' complaints. I better take it or she'll be bugging this place until she gets some kind of satisfaction." Joe held the phone to his ear. "Yes, Mrs. Ferris, this is Father Newman." His voice was most professional, but not his thoughts.

It seems that Joe was just the one on her mind. It was his sermon. She wanted to know how he, "a priest of God," could endorse these Jesus freaks who are just too lazy to get out and get a job. They couldn't hold a candle to the fine young people at St. Monica's who were living their Christian faith and doing real apostolic work. Joe explained that he wasn't knocking St. Monica's youth at all. All he said was that it was good to hear of kids turning off drugs and turning to Christ. This seemed to pacify her ... for the time being. Joe ended the conversation with, "I would love to discuss this with you, Mrs. Ferris, but I must go to the church now to baptize several infants. Let me compliment you: it's obvious you pay close attention to the sermons. Bye now." *(I'm in a bad frame of mind to welcome these tiny Christians into the fold.)* He looked at his watch as he walked briskly across the car lot to the Church. *(Great ... I'm running five minutes late. Hope these babies came equipped with full bellies and dry pants.)*

The church vestibule was filled with family and friends of the four babies. Joe made his apologies for being a little late, asked them to wait in one of the back pews by the baptistry then hurried to the sacristy to vest. He couldn't help but notice one of the godmothers was fumbling awkwardly with a crying infant; it didn't take an expert to know that she wasn't used to handling babies. *(Hope she brought a pacifier. Poor things, wrapped up in all that stiff lace and silk. Looks like they learn right from the very start the sacrifices they must make for their religion. There goes that sick feeling in my stomach.)*

On his way back to the baptistry, Joe noticed the little one had stopped crying; he was relieved. Joe still wanted more time to collect his thoughts before administering the sacrament so he knelt before the tabernacle to try to clear his mind that was racing with so many problems. He had promised to pray for Pam. Now was as good a time as any. Had he failed her when she needed help? How did the church lose her in the first place? *(We're losing kids all the time ... we're not getting through to them. We're losing priests, too ... and good ones at that, like Ed Pieri. What's going wrong, God?)*

During the first part of the baptismal rite Joe tried hard to concentrate. He let the parents and godparents take turns in reading the Scriptures and composing prayers, then preached a few words on the great miracle of baptism, the beginning of eternal life ... the birth of divine life. These babies were going to live forever. The words really struck him when he poured the water. Joe was a man and he worried like a man; but now he was an apostle continuing the work of Christ. Through his action of pouring water and these words, "I baptize you in the name of the Father and of the Son and of the Holy Spirit," someone lives forever. He took each baby in turn, still reflecting. Joe looked at his own hands pouring the water. *(This is where it all begins, right here in these apostolic hands: Christ is still speaking and acting and giving life in the twentieth century . . . and I am helping Him do it!)*

When the ceremony was finished, Joe received the usual invitations to the christening celebrations and exchanged small talk with the parents and godparents. They had to speak loud, however, for one baby, now Christopher Gerard, was bawling once again, while the young godmother became more and more nervous. The parents weren't present so they couldn't be of help in quieting the infant and the godfather was as afraid of the baby as she. Joe took the baby from her and put him to his shoulder, carefully supporting the baby's back and head. He swayed slowly, patting the little bottom gently. Soon the baby was quiet and appeared to be going to sleep. The very young godmother looked on in astonishment. "You should have a bunch of kids!" She realized her candid remark and the implications. "I mean you should *have had* a bunch of kids . . . I mean you would have made a terrific husband . . . I mean, Father . . . I mean it is really something the way you handle that baby." Soon she was stammering apologetically. "I mean I'll bet you had a lot of practice . . . baptisms and all!" she hastened to add. She was embarrassed.

Joe laughed at the girl's frenzy, but his smile soon changed to a look of anticipation as he felt a warm dampness penetrate his cassock and reach his skin. No rubber pants on this one, he thought, as he handed the sleeping infant back to the girl.

It was past eight o'clock when Joe pulled up to the traffic signal, reached for a cigarette, then pushed in the lighter. He was becoming more irritated by the long wait for the light to change. The lighter didn't pop out. He smashed the dashboard with the heel of his hand and began jiggling it furiously. It was

19

stuck. The traffic signal turned green; he slipped the clutch out too quickly and killed the motor. The driver behind him leaned on his horn. Joe wanted to answer the blare and was just about to when he remembered he was wearing his collar. He threw the unlit cigarette on the floor of the car and turned on the ignition. It stalled. The car behind continued to blast. With as much patience as he could muster, Joe motioned to the driver to go around him. By the time the car was ready to go, the light turned red again. He looked at his watch; it was 8:30 p.m., 8:30 and he was lost, tired, angry, *and*, he just realized, very hungry!

Joe had hoped to get an earlier start this evening, but Sunday was always one day he was never sure of just what would happen. He had said the 8:30 and 10 a.m. Masses and had helped with Communions at three other Masses, then baptisms at 3 p.m. As usual, he paid a visit to each of the christening parties. If he had gone to one and not to the others, it could cause hard feelings. He thought for sure, he would knock the last one out by six o'clock and he would have if he hadn't become involved in defending the new liturgy to two of the conservative godparents, who were upset because "the Catholic Church just wasn't what it used to be!" His plans early in the day to correct essay papers this evening were shot down; that meant he must take time out tomorrow for that chore. If he didn't get to St. Andrew's Methodist Church soon, he might never see Ed and he would have made this trip for nothing, wasting another valuable Sunday evening. *(Of all parts of town I have to pick this area to lose my way. My Roman collar could be a help or hindrance in these parts . . . never know how some may react. One thing is for certain: Ed didn't say* Grand *Street . . . there's not a church in sight! The smart thing to do would have been to check the address before I left, but then that would have been too simple.)* Joe slammed his hand against the steering wheel in disgust; he wasn't too sure of where *Grant* Street was either. He pulled alongside a young couple standing on a corner.

"Excuse me, can you tell me how to get to *Grant* Street from here?"

The young man, who looked more like a young lady, with his long hair, left the girl and walked idly toward the car. "Did you say *Grant?*" he said as he placed his hands on the car door and peered through the open window.

"Yes, *Grant* Street. I'm looking for St. Andrew's Methodist Church. You know where it is?" Joe questioned. He studied the boy. He looked like John the Baptist with his long shoulder-length hair, frayed clothes, and fast-and-abstinence look. Joe felt food wasn't the only thing this young man had abstained from. Soap and water must have been a rare commodity in his circles too.

"Yeah, I know where it's at, but you're a long way off." The boy moved in closer to the window. "At first, I thought you were a priest. That kind of collar threw me."

"I am a priest."

"And you're headin' for a Methodist church?"

Joe tried not to show his irritation. "Look, I'm in a hurry. Could you just tell me where it is?"

"Hey, man, I got a better idea. I'll drive with you. It ain't far from my house."

The boy moped around the front of the car, seeming to take forever. He opened the door of the passenger's side and slowly slinked in. "Let's move. Make a right," he said as he slumped in the seat.

"What about your girl friend?"

The boy laughed. "That ain't *my* girl friend. She's every-body's girl friend. You know what I mean? She's a hooker!" He watched Joe's reaction to see if he had shocked him. He hadn't.

After going a few blocks, Joe tried to break the awkward silence by switching on the radio. It was already set on a rock station and the wild sound of drums filled the car.

"Hey, man, you dig soul?"

"I dig it," Joe said as he grinned at his own stifled retort. 'Souls are my business.' " He knew the pun was too corny for this hippie type. "What's your name?"

"Gregg Bruno," the boy answered, bobbing his head in rhythm to the music, and added, "What's yours?"

"Father Newman. How far is the church from here?"

" 'Bout fifteen minutes. Soon as we get on the main street, you'll know where you're at." Gregg reached down to turn the volume lower. "I didn't mean to be cute back there when you told me you were a priest." His voice lost some of its previous belligerence. "I mean when you asked for a Methodist church, I thought maybe you were a minister or something, but I figured you were a priest soon as I saw your collar."

"Forget it."

"I used to be a Catholic — served Mass and everything."

"Used to be?" Joe questioned.

"Yeah. I ain't nothing now. Got turned off all that phony bull. All religions are alike. They preach that 'love your neighbor' stuff and smile at each other in church on Sunday, then crab at each other the rest of the week. Ain't that right?" Gregg was waiting for a reply; when he didn't get one, he looked closely at Joe. "Sorry about that. Didn't mean to knock your religion . . . but it is true. They are all the same."

"When did you turn off?"

"When I was sixteen — 'bout three years ago. My old lady threw a fit 'cause I dropped out of school. I moved out right after that."

"Are you living with your folks now?"

"Man, I ain't got no choice. I have to. I'm in big trouble . . . pot. Got caught with it. This is a bad scene, man. My folks got me a good lawyer though and he says I might be able to beat it if I play it cool."

"Were you pushing the stuff?" Joe asked.

"That's just it. I wasn't, but the guy I was with, was. The lawyer told me to move back home and get a job and start night school . . . you know, give the jury a good impression. Hell, I'm even getting a haircut!"

Joe pulled up to the red light and turned toward Gregg to study him for a minute; he watched him light a cigarette and draw in deeply. The light changed and he drove on.

Gregg leaned his head against the headrest, staring at the ceiling of the car. "Religion left me cold . . . couldn't feel it. Grass, now *that's* something I could feel. I could flip out on acid or get high on pot; it really turned me on. Know what I mean?" He dragged deeply again on his cigarette, then answered his own question, "No, I don't guess you do." Once again Gregg inhaled deeply; this time he held the smoke in for a few seconds until he noticed Joe was glancing at him rather suspiciously. "Hey, man, this ain't what you think it is. It's straight!" He reached in his jacket and retrieved a pack of cigarettes as if to give added proof. "Want a smoke?"

"Thanks," Joe answered and smiled a little apologetically as he reached for the cigarette protruding from the proferred pack.

"I'm off all that stuff now. Man, I had a couple of bad trips you wouldn't believe. I left the whole scene — drugs, freaking out, sex . . . the whole bag. I've had it."

"Seems like you're heading in the right direction, Gregg."

"I don't know where I'm heading. Could be jail if that lawyer ain't sharp enough. Hey, you don't mind me talking like this, do you? I mean I been kind of bombing your religion, but I just don't buy it."

"I haven't been trying to sell it, have I?" Joe answered as he drew in on his own cigarette.

"No. How come?"

"I figured you wanted a ride, not a sermon."

"Hey, man, you must be like some of those other priests that say hell and sin is just a lot of bull. Am I right?"

"Wrong. If I believed that, I wouldn't be wearing this collar. I'd be out living it up . . . no reason not to."

"I suppose," Gregg said thoughtfully, staring ahead. He looked at Joe seriously and it seemed he was about to say something else, but he just shrugged his shoulders and turned the volume back up on the radio as if to conclude the conversation.

Joe waited for more talk but it didn't come. It was obvious the boy was troubled, but how could he find the right words to get through to him? Joe had tried to effect a nonchalant attitude with Gregg, but he was, in fact, going through a thousand things in his mind and he was frightened to say really anything; it wouldn't take much to turn Gregg off, just as he had done earlier today with Pam.

Finally Gregg broke the silence. "You're just three blocks away from the church now. Make a right at the next corner and go two blocks."

"Where do you live? I'll drop you off first," Joe said as he

23

slowed down to the stop light, looking askance at the youth.

"Forget it. Let me out on the next corner." Gregg's voice had changed. He seemed despondent.

"I thought you wanted a lift home."

"Look, that was just a bunch of bull. Drop me off at the next corner. I don't live anywhere around here. I used to bum with some guys from this neighborhood; that's how come I knew where the church was."

"I don't get it." Joe paused for a moment. "Gregg, do you want me to help you in any way?" Joe knew now was the time to speak up. Gregg's aggressive attitude was now becoming quite different; he seemed agitated.

"There's nothing you can do. This is going to sound dumb, but I guess I just wanted someone to talk to. Did you ever get that way?"

"Lots of times. Do you want to talk now?"

"Right now? I thought you had to get to that church?"

"Those meetings last hours. I'll catch my friend before he leaves," Joe said as he pulled alongside the curb. The car was dimly illuminated by the huge billboard at the corner. Joe turned off the ignition and lights, pushed the lever to slide the seat back, and pivoted slightly toward Gregg. "Gum?" he asked as he offered the pack.

"Thanks," Gregg said stupidly, then half-smiled. "You're different. I never found a priest who just took time out to sit and talk."

"Maybe you never were looking for any before." Joe began to fold the stick of gum in his mouth. "You've got some big troubles, right?"

"Like I might end up in jail, or blow my mind . . . one of the two. Man, I'm screwed up." Gregg ran his fingers through his hair pushing his head back and slumping farther in the seat.

"I don't know how I can help you with your trouble with the law; but I may be able to help your frame of mind," Joe offered.

"I need some kind of help, Father. Man, I'm scared. I'm up to my neck with troubles and I don't know which way to turn. Like tonight I didn't want that broad back there, but she was just there so I figured, 'What the hell . . .'"

"Gregg, what you need is direction. Sometimes when we don't know where to take our troubles, we must turn to God and ask —"

"Hold on," Gregg interrupted defensively; "I thought you weren't going to give me no sermon."

"You hold on," Joe raised his voice impatiently. "You wanted to talk to someone and you made up that story about dropping you off at your house when you saw I was a Catholic priest. Now you tell me, if I were just some guy lost and you hadn't seen this collar, would you still have gone for the ride?"

"I don't know," Gregg said somewhat dejectedly, then began ringing his hands. "All I know is that I don't want to listen to a lot of crap I don't believe."

"What you call 'crap' is what others call faith, faith that Someone greater than ourselves can help us over the hump when we can't make it ourselves. Now, *that's* not crap. That's common sense," Joe answered angrily.

"Well, it don't make no sense to me and if you don't mind, preacher, I can get that kind of phony bull_____ from my old lady. See you around!" Gregg left the car and slammed the door.

Joe called to Gregg. When he didn't answer, Joe started to go after him; but as soon as Gregg heard the car door slam, he began to run. Joe stopped and watched the boy turn down a side street running at a startling pace. It almost appeared as if he were running away from something, that he was afraid. *(Blew that one. Me and my temper. Why couldn't I have just kept my mouth shut and listened for a little while longer!)* For the next few blocks, till he pulled up at St. Andrew's, Joe retraced the whole conversation in his mind, trying to understand what he said that led up to Gregg's abrupt departure.

The meeting was just breaking up as Joe entered the hall. He looked swiftly over the crowd, but he couldn't spot Ed Pieri. Joe recognized one of the priests that was walking toward him.

"Little late, aren't you, Joe?"

"I knew I couldn't make the meeting, but I was looking for Father Pieri. You know where he is?" Joe asked as he stretched to look through the assembly.

"He didn't make it, either. Missed a good meeting too."

25

"How come? You two usually drive to the meetings together, don't you?" Joe asked.

"That's right. And he usually phones first. When he didn't, I tried to reach him, but he was at the school hall . . . a dance or something. Figured he must be tied up and forgot to call." The priest looked at his watch. "Got to run, Joe. Sorry you made the trip for nothing. Take it easy."

"Yeah, you too," Joe answered as he walked toward the vice-chairman of the group, a Presbyterian, now engaged in conversation with a few other clergymen.

"Excuse me," Joe interrupted. "I thought Father Pieri would be here this evening and I wanted to talk to him. I see he didn't make it." Joe hoped he would hear why, without asking directly.

"No, Father Pieri didn't make it. I was surprised not to see him this evening. He had prepared a report for tonight and I know when I spoke to him yesterday afternoon, he was planning to present it. He didn't telephone either. He must have been called away for something important and didn't have time to call. That happens to all of us," the minister said with an amiable smile.

"I'm sure that's what happened," Joe agreed, then excused himself and started for the door. Joe wished he was certain that that was what really happened; however, he couldn't help but feel something wasn't right. Ed always took time to phone if he couldn't meet an appointment.

Ascension Rectory wasn't too far out of the way on Joe's way home and since it was getting close to eleven, he decided to stop for something to eat, then drive by Ed's to see if he may be there. The only cars in the rectory drive belonged to Ed's pastor, Monsignor Kamp and the other assistant, Father Schumacher. There was no sign of Ed. Joe followed a hunch and started for Ed's parents' home. It was only a ten-minute drive and there was no sense in going home; he knew he couldn't sleep anyway. It was no real sacrifice for Joe to drive to the Pieri home; he always thought best when driving and tonight he needed time to think and sort things out. This just wasn't like his best friend. It was always Ed who provided the support when Joe was in doubt;

he acted as a kind of stabilizer for Joe's sometimes feverish temper. *(Whatever is bothering Ed must be a real problem; he just isn't the type of guy who lets anything throw him.)*

To find no trace of Ed's car at his parents' was even more disturbing. All the lights were out in the Pieris' modest white cottage; it looked as if the couple had retired for the night. *Ed may have returned to the rectory by now.* Joe headed back toward Ascension. The lights were out and still just two cars in the drive. Joe parked his car about four houses down from the rectory, turned off his lights and sat back. *(He has to come home soon. He always has the seven o'clock weekday Masses. This is stupid. Ed may be any number of places and here I sit like some kind of spy waiting for my contact.)* Joe looked at the houses up and down the street; almost all were dark. He looked at his watch. Almost midnight. *(Where is he? Maybe his car broke down — that could be it. Just a few days ago he was complaining about the alternator being almost shot. He could be stuck somewhere, but where? But he still would have managed to get to a phone and tell them he wasn't showing up for the meeting. What if his car is in the shop now and he is fast asleep in the rectory while I'm sitting here like a fool freezing?)*

A car slowed down at the corner, but Joe couldn't make it out too clearly; the headlights were glaring in his eyes. Joe sat up and watched closely. If it were Ed, he would have to make a mad dash to catch him before he went to the door. All Ed would need is to have the "old man" hear him come in or hear any noise by the rectory. Joe sat back and folded his arms across his chest as the car passed the house. He argued with himself whether or not to go home; but he had waited this long. He might as well stick it out another half hour; but if Ed wasn't back by 12:30, he was leaving.

Joe put the lighter to his last cigarette, then leaned across the seat toward the glove box to see if he had a spare pack. He felt silly as he realized he was acting like an addict lining up his next fix. Gregg flashed back in Joe's mind, and along with the image came the frustration and confusion as to how to help kids like this who were turned off the Church and society, but turned on to drugs. Joe smoked the cigarette down to the bitter end; he looked like he was saying good-bye to a dear friend as he threw it out the window and watched it slowly die. That was two packs today . . . a lot for a Sunday. The whole morning was tied up in church and he never smoked then — only perhaps a cigarette between Masses. *(I must cut down! But why should I? I gave up everything else . . . don't drink, except socially once in a while. Can't afford to bowl as much as I used to — besides there's never enough time. Every celibate is entitled to one vice. Wonder if celibates smoke more than married people. According to some books about celibacy, many sublimate their human needs with tobacco, painting, sports, sometimes drink. I'm no Rembrandt, there's not enough spare time for sports, and drinking is far more dangerous morally to a priest than smoking.)* He talked himself into having another cigarette; but when he reached in his pocket he remembered he had just finished his last one. *(Well, I should cut down anyway.)*

Another car slowed to the corner but Joe immediately recognized it wasn't Ed's. He leaned back on the headrest and closed his eyes. He looked at his watch again . . . almost 12:30. *(Fifteen more minutes, then I'm going!)*

The rain drumming on the roof of the car woke Joe. He looked at his watch: it was almost three in the morning. He rubbed the back of his stiff neck and peered toward the rectory . . . still no sign of Ed's car. If only there were some way he could tell whether Ed was in there, he thought. Joe started the car, then turned the heater on; he was shivering as he pulled slowly toward the rectory. He looked at the window of what he knew was Ed's room; the shade was up. That told him something. Surely Ed would have pulled down the shade before he went to bed — if not for the sake of modesty, then simply not to get the early morning sun. Joe accelerated the car and headed for home.

Joe slipped the key in the lock and slowly opened the door; he held his hand gently on the large lock as he shut it behind him, then very, very, quietly he slipped off his shoes and crept down the hall towards his room. He could hear the deep snoring as he passed Father Benetti's room. It was 3:20 and that meant in less than three hours, he had to begin another day with seven o'clock Mass. As he began to undress, he saw a note on his bed.

He sat down and held the note close to the bedlamp, and began reading.

Joe,

Will you take the 8:00 Mass this week for me and I'll do your 7:00. I have to be at the university early all week. Msgr. Flannagan is feeling pretty bad so Benetti is taking the 6:00 for him. Thanks.

Peace,
George

"Terrific," Joe mumbled to himself as he reset his alarm clock, granting himself another full hour of sleep.

It was a comforting feeling lying in bed at last; but Joe couldn't sleep. His neck was still stiff from his awkward position in the car and there was too much on his mind. Had anything gone right today? He had annoyed people more than usual with his sermon. He really hadn't got through to Pam. Gregg had walked out on him and he couldn't even get Ed to listen to him. *(God, why did You pick me for the priesthood?)* He turned on his side and pulled the cover around his shoulders as he snuggled deeper in the pillow. Joe felt an anxious feeling in the pit of his stomach. He tried to pray but words wouldn't come. Even God wasn't listening. *(God, why did You pick me? What a day. What did I do wrong? Did I really help anyone today?)* The questions kept coming . . . then sleep.

CHAPTER 2

WHAT'S SO SPECIAL?

(Monday)

The enrollment at St. Monica's parish school was too large to have the complete student body attend Mass every morning, so a few classes were assigned different days of the week. Joe had the seventh and eighth grades for the eight o'clock Mass today. He had difficulty in concentrating during the liturgy; aside from the fact that Gregg Bruno and Father Ed were still on his mind, the giggling and escapades of two eighth-grade boys offered further distraction. When Joe first approached the altar and presented the theme of the Mass, "What makes you so special?" he noticed the two were beet-red trying to stifle their laughs. And later when he called upon the congregation to examine their consciences as he was running over in his mind his own weaknesses — bad temper, loss of patience, lack of trust — his attention was completely shifted to the third pew where he noticed the boys were passing notes. Finally before he began his homily, he was so completely distracted by the pair, he decided to stop and directly address them.

"Boys, what was the theme of the Mass today? I'm talking to you, Mark and Steve!" His voice was stern. Both boys lifted their flushed faces toward the pulpit, but neither answered. Joe repeated the question, "I'll ask again. What was the theme of today's Mass?" Again, no reply.

Joe leaned forward. "Perhaps if you had been paying attention, you would have been able to answer. For your benefit, I'll repeat it. The theme of the Mass is: 'What makes you so special?' Now if you will, I would like to have your attention during the homily; unless of course, you feel you don't need it . . . in which case, I ask, 'What makes you so special?' "

For the next ten minutes the pair never took their eyes from Joe. They listened closely as Joe explained that baptism "made them special," and throughout the rest of the liturgy, both boys never so much as glanced away from the altar.

When Joe returned to the rectory, Mrs. Quinlan was busy in the kitchen setting his place at the table. Most of the time Dearie seemed quite calm regardless of what chaos existed, between the ringing of the telephone and the rectory doorbell. She was a short, stout woman with a round face that displayed an almost perpetual smile. This morning though she seemed unusually concerned. Joe took his place at the table as she directed; she began to pour his coffee when he heard a hissing noise coming from the stove. A thick foaming something-or-the-other was erupting under the lid of the small pot. "My Lord, there goes Monsignor's breakfast," she yelled as she hurried to retrieve the angry contents from the stove.

"What's that stuff?" Joe asked, silently relieved that it wasn't *his* breakfast.

"Cream of wheat . . . and it's very good and nourishing, especially if you have ulcers."

"Is Monsignor still feeling bad?"

"Terrible! Father Benetti took the six o'clock Mass. Poor Monsignor hasn't even left his room . . . and you know how he is about his morning coffee and paper. I tell you, Father Joe, he is very ill . . . can't keep a thing on his stomach. The poor man's practically down to nothing."

Father Benetti entered the kitchen, poured himself a cup of tea, nodded to Joe over his spectacles and started back for his room.

"Good morning, Father," greeted Joe.

"How's that?" Father Benetti responded.

"I said, 'Good morning,' " Joe repeated in a louder voice.

"Certainly is," the old priest answered, then returned to his room. Almost every morning you could find the old priest doing

31

the same thing, reading his office to the soft Italian operas playing in the background. The old man treasured his record collection, but Joe could never remember ever hearing anything in English; everything was in Italian.

Joe didn't even wait to finish his breakfast; as soon as Dearie left to bring Monsignor Flannagan his tray, he pivoted in his chair and began to dial Ed Pieri on the wall phone.

"Ascension Rectory." It was the housekeeper, Mrs. Burke.

"Good morning, Mrs. Burke!" Joe said in mock cheerfulness: he knew this irritated her. "Is Father Pieri there, dear?"

"I don't know if he is or not," was her reply, followed by complete silence.

Joe waited for a second and was just about to ask if someone was still there when he heard her shrill voice. "Father Pieri here?"

Dearie walked back into the kitchen; Joe shielded the receiver with his free hand and whispered to Dearie, "That old gal takes ugly pills — Old Lady Burke, I mean." He motioned toward the phone.

"Shame on you, Father. Mrs. Burke has had much misery in her life."

"She's caused a lot too," Joe answered as he reached for his coffee.

Dearie giggled, then turned to Joe with a chastising look.

Finally Ed came to the phone. It was obvious by the tone of his voice that he was still upset. He explained to Joe that he couldn't talk because his pastor was in the other room and things were very tense. Joe arranged to meet Ed at Tony's Restaurant for a pizza and a beer at two that afternoon.

"Monsignor Flannagan asked for you to come see him in his room when you have a free minute, Father Joe," Dearie said as she cleared the table.

Joe went directly to the pastor's room where the monsignor was seated at a small desk. "Good morning. Feeling any better?"

"I was, till I got up and decided to go over a little bookwork. Bills!" he said, holding up a fistful of papers.

Monsignor Flannagan was a tall man in his middle sixties; his hair was almost totally white, giving him a very distinguished appearance. For the most part, he was very easy to get along with and Joe had found his association with his pastor quite compatible. Although Monsignor Flannagan admitted that he was basically a conservative, and preferred the "old ways," he was nevertheless ready to listen to new ideas, a trait Joe admired in him. Even George Rahner, the junior assistant, had to admit that their pastor was a fair man — quite a concession coming from such a liberal and rebel as George. Monsignor Flannagan had a keen wit also. When his parishioners teased him about his devotion to the golf course, he would simply reply: "I have two loves in my life — God and golf . . . but always in that order!"

The pastor swiveled his chair around to face Joe; he grew quite serious. "Joe, you know I've never put any restrictions on you, or any of my assistants . . . and I'm not going to now. I trust your judgment. Normally, I would just dismiss something like this, but under the present circumstances I know you are going to be called upon to take over quite a bit of the load at St. Monica's, for a while at least. I'm not feeling up to it right now. It's this lousy stomach," he said as he gripped himself under the right rib. "What I'm saying, Joe, is that it's important that you have the respect and cooperation of the parish. I know you're well-liked here, and you're doing a good job, but it takes one instance like this, and you could have big trouble."

"I don't know what instance you're talking about," Joe said as he took a chair. He was bewildered.

"I'm certain there's a simple explanation for it, Joe, but I received a call from someone early this morning while you were at Mass. I wouldn't have even taken the call, except that you and George were gone and the caller insisted that it was imperative that she speak with someone in charge. She claimed that you were seen last night in a parked car with a girl in the heart of town. You know what she's talking about, Joe?"

"I wasn't with any girl last night. In fact, I spent most of the evening with some teen-age boy I picked up to help me find —" Suddenly it dawned on Joe. He and Gregg had been seen in the car, and in the half-darkness, Gregg could easily have been mistaken for a girl with his shoulder-length hair. Joe grinned, then explained the situation to Monsignor Flannagan. The elder priest assured Joe that he had imagined it was something like this, but cautioned him always to exercise prudence. Neither of the two men knew the caller as she didn't identify herself. The thought of someone not hesitating to draw a conclusion and rushing to report his whereabouts bothered him. He wished he knew who it was and prayed silently that this story would not go any farther than the caller, but that was doubtful.

Monsignor Flannagan gave Joe a few instructions about the upcoming Ladies' Guild night, then reminded him to call Sister Jeanine, the principal, if he had to be called away and could not hold his religion classes. She had called the pastor to ask Joe to "extend this courtesy, as she had a school to run, and organization was most important to her!"

"Is there anything else, Monsignor?" Joe asked.

"Just one more thing." The pastor hesitated; he seemed reluctant to ask his next question. "Do you and George spend much time together? I mean . . . do you ever just talk?"

"Not really. George is gone quite a bit. Seems like when I'm in, he's out." Joe couldn't understand the unusual question, but from the look on the monsignor's face, it must have been an important one. "Why do you ask?"

"I thought perhaps you could enlighten me a little. I know George is active in many of the social groups around town — civil rights, the anti-war organization, and such. And of course, he has his classes at the university which take up a great deal of his time. The truth is, I scarcely see him around here. Do you think he's happy at St. Monica's?"

"He's never expressed that he was, or was not," Joe answered blankly.

"He does his job. I mean he's right on time for the Masses, but unless I requested it, he's never attended one parish meeting in the year he's been at St. Monica's. He's hardly ever around, except occasionally at the evening meals and then his conversation is never about anything pertaining to the parish." The monsignor rested back in his chair and looked at Joe. The seriousness left his voice. "At any rate, Joe, I was just wondering. Forget I mentioned it."

34

Joe went to his room to start correcting the essay papers he had planned to do the night before. He lit a cigarette and began to fumble through the papers. He wasn't in the mood for fifth-grade essays when there were so many other things on his mind. *(Strange ... that's the first time Flannagan ever mentioned to me anything about George. Must be worried about him. Maybe he had a call about him too? No wonder the old man has ulcers: I'm supposed to be messing around with some gal and George is ... George is what? Never really thought about it much until now, but George seldom talks about much of anything, anything about himself, that is ...)*

It was 2:15 when Joe arrived at Tony's Restaurant; Ed was already seated at a corner table. Definitely Italian in appearance, he was slightly built, not quite five feet, eight inches tall; the only feature he inherited from his Irish mother was his light hazel eyes, and although he was thirty-four, he looked much younger.

"You're late. I ordered a large sausage pizza, okay?" Ed asked as Joe sat down. The waiter brought a schooner of beer to the table. "You want the same, Father?" Joe nodded "yes" to the waiter.

"Warm for October ... didn't even need this sweater," Ed said, pulling the sleeve of his green cardigan.

"I didn't come to discuss the weather," Joe replied as he reached in his jacket for a cigarette.

"How come you're not wearing civvies?" Ed asked. "Everybody here knows you're a priest," he added mirthfully with a broad grin.

"I didn't have time to change ... got hung up on answering a parlor call. What am I doing explaining anything to you? You call me yesterday, tell me you're leaving the priesthood, and like a fool, I try to track you down and end up spending half the night sitting in the car waiting for you." Joe stopped as the waiter approached with his beer. As soon as the waiter was out of earshot, he continued, "How come you didn't get to St. Andrew's last night?"

"Something came up."

"I went to St. Andrew's just when the meeting was closing, then I headed for your place —"

"For God's sake," Ed interjected anxiously, "you didn't go to the door, did you?"

"Of course not! I parked down the street and watched the drive. It was almost three when I left. Where were you?"

"I was with Ellen. I didn't get back to the rectory till almost seven this morning. The old man knows it too. I didn't even go into the house — just went straight to Church and said Mass."

Joe was angry at the way Ed so nonchalantly announced he had been with a girl all night, then calmly proclaimed that he went back to say Mass. What baffled him more was that Joe had never heard any mention of "Ellen" till now. Maybe he didn't know his best friend so well after all. Joe sipped his beer and tried to muster up enough patience to speak calmly to his friend.

"That was big of you, Ed, managing to get back to say the seven, really big of you." Joe was sarcastic.

"Spare me the lecture. I got enough of that from the old man this morning." Ed downed his beer, then motioned to the waiter to bring him another.

"Fill me in, will you? Who is this Ellen?"

"She's the head of the teen choir . . . great gal."

Joe sat there staring at Ed for a few seconds before shaking his head disgustedly and asking, "How long has this been going on?"

"What are you talking about? Nothing's 'going on,' as you put it. I just talked with her till about two when I dropped her off at her place. I drove around for — God knows how long, then stopped at an all-night diner and had coffee. I went by my sister's house to clean up before I went back to church for Mass."

"If nothing's going on, how did you manage to be with her till two in the first place? Is she so important you couldn't even call to let the people at St. Andrew's know you weren't coming?" Joe realized he was raising his voice. He took a deep drag from his cigarette.

"If you would quit sounding off, maybe I'd have a chance to tell you what happened. I didn't call anybody last night because I was uptight. Any doubts I may have had about leaving the priesthood were certainly gone after last night. That old man embarrassed me to the point that I — " Ed stopped when he saw the waiter coming toward them with the pizza.

When the waiter left, Joe picked up the thread of conversation, this time in a calmer voice. "I don't understand you, Ed. You're a good priest, you get through to people I wouldn't think would give you the time of day. You've always been the one reminding me to think twice before I act."

"I know all that . . . but it's not enough. Joe, I feel like a machine. Push the right button and I'll do what I'm told. The Church is unreal."

"We all feel like that sometimes, but —"

"But nothing!" Ed interrupted vehemently. "I'm a man! I want to feel like one."

"Does this Ellen have anything to do with this?" Joe asked, hoping he would hear the right answer.

"Not exactly."

"What do you mean? Either she does or she doesn't!" *(There goes my temper again.)*

Ed took a deep breath before replying. "I haven't done anything. I just told you that. The only time I've ever been alone with her until last night was in church when we were getting the folk songs ready for the teen group. That's the whole point, Joe; she looks at me like I'm a black cassock, a white collar and a face with a big tattoo on my forehead saying, 'Don't touch, I'm a priest.' When I talk to her, she looks right through me, not at me."

"Start from the beginning. Who is she?"

"She's in the parish, about twenty-three, or around there. She works at one of the utilities downtown, but she studied music in college and she volunteered to help me with the folk group. You should see what she's done with those kids, singing in three-part harmony and everything. Well, she's been coming one night a week to help out for about the past three months. She's not pretty, Joe, but there's something about her. She's warm, feminine . . . I don't know exactly how to explain it. But when I'm with her, she makes me feel like a man. You know what I mean?"

37

Joe shrugged. "Does she know how you feel?"

"That's what I'm telling you . . . she looks at me as if I were one of the marble statues in the church. She treats me as if I were some kind of god."

"Then you really aren't involved with her in any way?" Joe said, relieved.

"I don't even know her very well, but I like her. Maybe that's why I blew up last night like I did, because I was embarrassed in front of her." Ed lifted a piece of pizza from the tray. "Better start eating . . . it's getting cold."

"You're something else! I'm still waiting to hear about what happened last night and all you're worried about is your pizza getting cold!" Joe looked up to see an almost hurt expression on Ed's face. "Sorry, go on," Joe apologized, taking a bit of pizza to please Ed; but he was too upset to really enjoy it.

"Last night," began Ed between bites of pizza, "the teen group was having a dance in the hall. So before I started to get ready to go to St. Andrew's for the meeting, I figured I'd run over and make sure everything was set up and they had enough chaperones. When I got over there, Ellen was at the door and we started to talk. It was a little windy out there, so we decided to go into the hall and you know what she did?"

"What?" Joe asked anxiously.

"She held the door open for me. *She held it open for me.* I'm a man! A man's supposed to hold a door open for a lady. But not a priest. A priest is supposed to bow politely and accept all the courtesies given to him by a lady." Ed's voice began to rise steadily like mercury in a thermometer on a hot day. "He's not a man! He's a body and mind programmed to do the right things at the right time! Push the button and do what you're told!"

"Calm down . . . you're not even making sense," Joe said quietly.

"Well, she made me sick when she did that." Ed almost sounded like a little boy. "I wanted to show her I was a man. Probably if she hadn't held that door open and I hadn't been so embarrassed by the janitor waiting there to tell me the old man was looking for me because I forgot to put the baptismal sacramentals away, I wouldn't have blown up like I did."

Ed wiped his mouth with the napkin, took a sip of beer, then continued. "You see, while I was talking to Ellen, I saw a couple of kids come in whom I didn't recognize. They were dressed like bums; they were filthy. When the one turned around, I spotted a flask in his back pocket. You know how you have to watch out for booze getting into these dances. So I went over and told him to give it to me. I told him he couldn't be admitted. He started to lip off, really belligerent. I told him to get out. I was still wearing my cassock. When he turned to leave, he said something to his buddy about the 'fag in the black dress.' I belted him; it caught him off guard and he fell. That drew a crowd and a couple of chaperones came running over. He was still on the floor. I started to help him up, but he pulled away. Instead of being mad, he began to laugh. The chaperones and I walked him toward the door. He looked back at me and said, laughing the whole time, 'If it ain't the Blessed Virgin!' I'm telling you, Joe, I almost went after him again."

"Did the boss find out?"

"You kidding? He was over in the hall within minutes yelling, in front of everybody too, 'Father Pieri, I'll see you outside!' I stepped outside the door, then he started yelling at me like I was some kid. Told me he was putting me on curfew and that I had better start shaping up.

"Ellen was standing right by the door . . . she heard every word he said. I didn't even answer him. I just took off across the school yard and headed for my car. Ellen followed me. She asked where I was going, and I told her I didn't know or care. So she asked if she could come along, saying maybe I just needed someone to talk to, that I was in no frame of mind to be driving a car. I took my cassock off and threw it in the back seat because I had a sweater under it. When I turned around, Monsignor Kamp was still standing by the doorway of the hall. He watched me drive off with Ellen. For all he knows I could have been with her till seven this morning. To tell you the truth, Joe, I don't give a damn what he thinks. Not any more. I'm getting out!"

"Where did you go from there?"

"To Ellen's uncle's place. He has a small restaurant. We had a couple cups of coffee, talked, then left and drove around and talked some more till I dropped her off, about two-thirty."

"What did you talk about?" Joe asked rather suspiciously.

"Mostly about what happened. I told her how fed up I was and what my plans were. She told me that I shouldn't let something like this get me down . . . said she was going to offer her Masses and Communions for me. I felt like a heel. She kept telling me about what a great priest I am and all I wanted to do was grab her and tell her I was a man, too!"

Joe hesitated before he asked the next question. "Did you?"

"Of course not!" Ed answered disgustedly. "Don't you see, Joe? All this last night wouldn't have happened if I hadn't been so uptight to begin with." Ed folded his napkin, leaving almost the entire pizza untouched. He lit another cigarette. "Look, Joe, we've been friends for a long time. Try and understand. I'm not with it anymore. I can't be a good priest anymore. I'd be better off out, and so would the Church. This weekend just kind of clinched it for me. Half the time the old man and I don't even speak. Joe, haven't you ever felt like you just wanted to think and act and feel like yourself, like a man, not a priest? You know what I'm talking about? For God's sake, say something!" There was real anxiety in Ed's voice and it was loud enough to attract the attention of a nearby table of women.

"I know how you feel . . . we all feel like that sometimes, but we get over it. You can still be your own kind of man." Joe's voice was very low; he didn't want to attract more attention. "Is celibacy what is getting to you most right now?"

"That and everything else. It's not just celibacy. We all knew what we were letting ourselves in for when we were ordained, but I'm not certain that I still feel that way. People change . . . I've changed. I'm trying to be honest with myself . . . and I've got to admit that I'm just not cutting it in the priesthood."

"I don't know what to say to you, but I do know this: you should talk to someone before you take any steps to see the bishop." Joe felt helpless; he couldn't find the right words to help Ed.

"It won't do any good, no matter whom I talk to. My mind's made up, Joe." Ed pressed out his cigarette as if he were pressing out any more of Joe's advice.

"Be back in a minute," Joe said, rising from his chair.

"Where you going?"

"To the john." *(If I tell him the truth, that I want to call Father Schumacher at the retreat house, he'll object; besides if Schumacher's not there, it will not have done any good anyway.)*

Joe went straight to the phone; it was out of Ed's view. As he was checking the number in the directory, he questioned if he was doing the right thing or not. *(But I have to do something. I just can't sit back and watch him walk out.)* Joe found the number and dialed quickly, praying that Father Schumacher would be there.

"What kept you?" Ed asked as Joe slid back into his chair.

"I called Father Schumacher. He said if you come out to the retreat house tomorrow some time, he can put you up for a few days. It will give you time to think things out." Joe lit another cigarette. "You remember him. He's the guy who gave the priests' retreat a couple of years ago. He's supposed to deal with priests' problems all the time —"

"I know who he is," Ed broke in impatiently. "What did you tell him?"

"I gave him a quick rundown . . . told him you were undecided about leaving. He said maybe a few days away from the whole scene may do you some good. What do you think?" Joe was hoping Ed would agree while he watched his friend's every expression.

"I just can't get through to you. I have decided and I told you what I'm going to do." Ed motioned to the waiter across the room for the check.

"You don't throw away half a lifetime just like that. For God's sake, see him, talk to him. So maybe you won't change your mind, but at least get somebody's advice," Joe urged.

"I don't know," Ed said, seeming to weaken a little. "Maybe I could do with a few days' rest, if nothing else."

"Then you'll call him and make the arrangements?"

"All right, all right, I'll call him," Ed answered in an aggravated tone. "But I'm telling you, Joe, my mind *is* made up!"

When Joe returned to the rectory, Dearie informed him that Mrs. Ferris had called twice. A few minutes later, Joe found himself listening once again to the litany of complaints, then the suggestions to remedy them. She felt the youth club should concentrate on a project for the Children's Hospital and cut out some of their dances. The Ladies' Guild should be making plans for the card party. And the Men's Club should cut out all that drinking after their meetings. Joe listened to her babble as he doodled on the desk pad; it was a stick lady, the head was extremely large to accommodate the gigantic mouth. *(Why does Monsignor Flannagan always leave her to me?)*

Finally when he couldn't take any more, Joe interrupted, "Why don't you present all your suggestions at the next Ladies' Guild, Mrs. Ferris? You know they are always looking for new ideas and I'm sure they would welcome them, coming from such a conscientious parishioner as yourself. I wish I could talk with you longer, but I am quite busy. Thank you for calling, dear. God bless you." Joe hung up the phone. He sat at his desk a few minutes. He was good at handling Mrs. Ferris. *(Terrific. That's somewhat of a simple task; but when it comes to real problems like Gregg Bruno's and Ed's, even Pam's . . . I always have to refer them to someone else. Is this my greatest talent as a priest — placating charming, rich, middle-aged, complaining women?)* The speculation disturbed him.

Dearie knocked on the office door and exclaimed in a loud voice, "Father, I forgot the most important thing. Your brother Tim called and asked to have you get in touch with him as soon as you came in. Sorry, Father, it slipped my mind."

"Thanks, Dearie, I'll call him right away," Joe answered as he dialed his brother's number and waited.

"Hello, Newman rez'dence. Timmy speakin'." Timmy's diction left much to be desired; but for only four years old, Joe admired how well he took directions regarding telephone manners.

"Hi, Timmy. This is Uncle Joe. Let me talk to your Daddy."

"Hi, Uncle Joe. Ya comin' t'ar house t'night? I gotta new football."

"That's nice. I'll come over and we'll play with it, but not tonight, Timmy. Maybe later in the week. Now, let me talk to your Daddy."

"What ya doin'?"

"I'm awfully busy, Timmy. Now let me talk to Daddy." Joe was trying not to become impatient with his nephew, but he wasn't in the mood for childish chatter.

"I watched Romper Room an' ya know what?"

"No, Timmy, what?" Joe conceded.

"There was a p'liceman on, jus' like Daddy, only he didn't have on the same kinda hat that Daddy wears an' . . ."

"Timmy, honey, listen to me," Joe interrupted.

"What d'ya want?"

"Tell me about it some other time, honey. Now, let me talk to your Daddy, okay?"

"Can't. He ain't home. He went to the doctor's. Susie's our baby-sitter. D'ya know 'er?"

"Is somebody sick, Timmy?"

"Jus' Mama . . . she keeps frowin' up alla time an' it mus' hurt 'cause she cries a lot when she frows up!" *(God, I hope it's the stomach flu! Kate couldn't take another one right now.)*

"D' ya wanna talk to Susie, Uncle Joe? I'll get 'er."

Before Joe could answer, Timmy was gone. The noise from the other end of the phone was unbelievable with Jeffrey, the three-year-old, screaming at Michael, the two-year-old, who was protesting loudly, and Paddy, the baby, wailing at the top of her lungs.

"Hello," bellowed Susie, trying to be heard above the din.

Joe found himself yelling back. "It's Father Joe; just tell my brother I was returning his call. I'll get back to him some time tonight. You got that?"

"Yes, Father, I'll tell him. Bye."

When Joe took his place at the dinner table, he noticed the pastor's place wasn't set; however, George's was. Dearie explained that Monsignor Flannagan was just having some broth in his room since the condition of his stomach wouldn't allow him to dine at the table. George rushed in excitedly and began waving a paper at Father Benetti and Joe. "Take a look at this! They're expecting an anti-war demonstration in front of the chancery office tomorrow. They're protesting the fact that the Church isn't taking action in —"

"Who's protesting?" Father Benetti interrupted with seeming indifference as he casually reached for the ice water.

"A couple of different groups. It says here that they expect a number of priests from the area to participate." There was no reply from either of the two other priests. "Don't you see what this means?" George continued. "They are finally *doing* something!"

Joe asked George a few questions about the upcoming demonstration while Father Benetti remained silent, calmly eating his dinner. George not only narrated the complete article almost word for word, but added his own appraisal and approval. George wanted everyone to share his enthusiasm; he looked at Father Benetti who still remained expressionless, chomping on his food. "Did you hear what I was saying, Father?" George said loudly.

"I heard."

"Well?" George questioned impatiently.

Benetti said nothing; he merely shrugged his shoulders and reached for the bread.

"I don't believe he's real," George murmured under his breath. Joe hurried to change the subject.

Later the three priests retired to the den. George turned on the T.V., Father Benetti took his usual chair and began reading the paper, while Joe turned his direction toward the screen. There was a panel of doctors, housewives, students and one priest, discussing ecology and the population explosion. One of the students brought up the question of birth control.

"Here we go again," George said as he leaned forward in his chair to listen more closely to the priest's reply. The priest seemed to dodge the issue at first, but then went into a long defense on the Pope's position. The panel was definitely divided, but only one housewife agreed totally with the conservative stand of the priest. Joe stopped listening when the abortion topic was brought up; he had no doubts about this being *murder*. His own thoughts took over. *(Where do I stand? Do I really believe what the official Church expects of me? I give the impression I do. Only last week I spent an hour defending the sanctity of life and the courage required of a Christian in upholding the natural law . . . God's law. I say these things, but do I really believe . . .*

44

deep down in my very being? Do I really believe with my heart, or just my head? Conservative priests have no problems with it.) Joe glanced at Father Benetti who seemed completely oblivious to the dialogue coming from the T.V. *(But I'm not a real conservative, or a real liberal either.)* He looked toward George. *(What are my motives? Am I concerned with truth or popularity?)*

The lively discussion was interrupted by a commercial. On the screen came the picture of a girl, clad in a very skimpy bikini, walking toward the camera. She smiled sweetly and explained that she owed her healthy teeth and fresh breath to "X" toothpaste. The camera then panned a full shot of her most curvaceous figure as she turned slowly, looking over her shoulder seductively, and slinked away.

"Get that, Joe. Must be some toothpaste!" George said, never taking his eyes from the screen. The two younger priests began to laugh as Father Benetti looked at the screen and then at his colleagues over his spectacles. He nodded disapprovingly and went back to his paper.

For the next hour and a half, Joe tried to reach his brother, Tim, but each time his call was answered by a busy signal. Finally, when it was nearly 9 p.m. he announced to Mrs. Quinlan that he was going to run over to his brother's home. Father Benetti had already retired to his room and George had left to attend some meeting. Joe was too restless for T.V., and he was certain, in his frame of mind, he could not concentrate on reading. Besides, he needed the fresh air and driving at night relaxed him.

All the lights were on in Tim's house when Joe pulled in the drive. He rang the doorbell; in a few minutes the door swung open and there was three-year-old Jeffrey, standing nude and soaking wet. "Hi!" was his simple greeting.

"What are you doing running around at this hour? And look at you. You want to catch cold?" Joe scolded as he closed the door behind him. The commotion was tremendous. He could hear his brother shouting for Timmy to sit down in the tub, and for Michael to quit splashing. Jeff ran back towards the bathroom.

"Get in here! What are you doing running around like that?" Tim yelled at his son.

"He opened the door for me," Joe shouted back in Jeffrey's defense. He stood at the bathroom door. "Having fun?" he asked his brother laughingly.

"Fun, hell! Grab a towel and dry these kids off. I have to get the baby's bottle off the stove. The damn thing's probably boiling by now. I didn't hear the doorbell ring," he said as he left the bathroom, his arms covered with suds to the elbows.

"How could you, with all this noise?" Joe grabbed a towel and began with Jeffrey. "Here Timmy, you can help yourself . . . I'll get the spots you miss. Where's your pajamas?"

"Unner my pillow. I'll get 'em," he said and ran out of the bathroom dripping suds in his path.

"Who has been on the phone all this time, Tim?" Joe shouted to his brother.

"Nobody, not since supper."

"I've been trying to get you since seven," Joe explained. He took a set of pajamas from Timmy and started putting them on Jeff. "Timmy, get dried before you put yours on."

Tim was standing in the doorway holding Paddy, the six-month-old. "God, I just remembered Jeff went downstairs. . . . I'll bet he's got the phone off the hook again. Here!" he said, pushing the baby into Joe's arms. She began to cry again. Joe could hear his brother shouting from the basement. "Jeff, how many times have we told you to keep your hands off that phone? Now, all of you, get in bed!"

"What about our snack, Daddy?" Timmy called.

"Joe, get them a cookie, will you? I have to get this bottle cool," Tim said as he ran up from the basement.

"Where's the cookies, pal?" Joe asked Timmy.

"I'll show ya," he answered as he ran toward the kitchen. Joe followed, still trying to calm Paddy.

"Where's your Mama?"

"Frowin' up and cryin' in her room," Timmy answered indifferently as he reached in the cookie jar on the counter and began to distribute them to his brothers.

"Go to bed, boys. You can say your prayers by yourselves tonight," Tim directed as he ran the cool water over the filled baby bottle. "Jeff, go to the bathroom before you go to bed . . . and no more drinks." He turned to Joe. "Wets the bed," he explained.

"Takes after his father. You did it till you were about seven," Joe laughed.

"Thanks a lot. That's just what he needed to hear. Now if he's too lazy to get up, he'll just lay there and go. You're a big help."

"What's wrong with Kate?" Joe asked, although he felt he already knew.

"Guess," Tim answered disgustedly.

"I thought so. Should I go in there and talk to her?"

"You can try. She won't let me near her. All she's been doing is crying. The doctor gave her some tranquilizers to take but she said she won't take them because she's afraid they'll hurt the baby. I'm worried, Joe. She's never acted like this before." Tim took the baby from his brother. "Come in the living room. We can talk in there."

"I'll go in and listen to the boys' prayers, then I'll be right in," Joe said as he went down the hall to the boys' room.

As he knelt at their bottom bunk, he pretended to listen to the boys' prayers, but he was in fact thinking of what he could say to console his younger brother and Kate. Things hadn't been easy on them — married just five years and now expecting their fifth child. He kissed the boys, lifted Timmy in the top bunk and started out the door when Timmy called after him. "Forgot to bless us."

"Sorry, tiger." Joe lifted his hand for the blessing.

Tim was in an easy chair feeding Paddy her bottle when Joe walked in. "Fix us a drink, Joe. The stuff's in the cabinet over the sink. I need one."

"How far is she?" Joe asked as he reentered carrying the drinks.

"Almost three months. Can you beat that? Paddy will only be a year when she's due again. God, Joe, it's not that I don't want a baby. It's just that I can't see how I can keep up with everything on a cop's salary. And look what it's doing to Kate. The Pope and his damn encyclicals!"

"Maybe your promotion will come through," Joe said, offering consolation.

47

Tim dismissed the speculation with a shrug. "I've decided to get a vasectomy, Joe. I know what the Church says, but what do *you* say?"

"That's kind of a drastic step, isn't it?" Joe answered, dodging his brother's real question.

"What can be more drastic, as you put it, than your wife having a baby every year because she's too scrupulous to use something or take the pill?" Tim argued.

"If she's that hung up about birth control, what do you think her reaction will be when she finds out what you're planning to do?"

"I won't tell her if I can help it. Besides, I know what she feels deep down or she wouldn't be in there all torn up right now. This is the only way. I'm sure of it." Tim leaned the baby forward to burp. "You didn't answer my first question, Joe. What do you think?"

"As a priest, you know what I have to say, Tim. I think — "

"I didn't ask you 'as a priest.' I asked you as a brother!" Tim cradled the baby back in his arm and fed her the rest of the bottle. "Forget I brought it up. I don't want to tie up your conscience," he said in a voice tinged with bitterness.

Joe downed the rest of his drink. "I have a few bucks put away that I've been saving for tires. Could you use it?" Joe wanted to offer some kind of help since he had offered little consolation.

"No, but thanks," Tim smiled. "I'm sorry I put you on the spot. Maybe you could see Kate for a few minutes; maybe she'll talk to you." Tim sounded almost despondent.

Joe knocked gently on the bedroom door. "Kate, it's Joe. You still awake?"

"Come in, Joe," she answered in a muffled tone.

Kate was lying across the double bed; her eyes were swollen and red. "I know what you're going to say, Joe, about accepting God's will and all that and I know I'm really acting badly. I should be thankful my kids are all healthy and so am I, but I'm just so tired of diapers and baby bottles, and maternity clothes and . . ." Her words trailed off as she began sobbing again.

"Go ahead and cry if it makes you feel better." Joe sat down

48

beside her on the bed and patted her head as if he were comforting a child. She sat up and put her arms around him and literally cried on his shoulder. There as he held his sister-in-law closely to him, he tried to imagine what it would be like if Kate were his wife and this was his situation. Surely he would feel rotten knowing she had to go through this because they had loved each other when the calendar forbade it. He could sympathize with Tim's feeling at this moment. Kate was a beautiful woman, full of life, warm, sensitive; but now she was a little girl holding on to her guardian because she fell down and skinned her knee. This wasn't the kind of hurt that went away by merely kissing it. Joe wanted to say something . . . but what? There were no right words. All he could think of was, "Cry and get it out of your system, Kate," and held her while she did . . .

The loud soul music that filled the car when Joe switched on the radio didn't fit his mood; he changed the station. Joe felt a certain tension that seemed to be brought on by a feeling of guilt. He was glad he was leaving his brother's house with all the noise, the turmoil, the crying. He felt a definite security — or was it escape? — by the fact that he was returning to the rectory. The strains of a familiar song began on the radio. The soft orchestration was soothing until the chorus began to sing, "What kind of fool am I . . . who never fell in love? It seems that I'm the only one that I have been thinking of. What kind of man is this? An empty shell? An empty shell in which a lonely heart . . ." The rest of the song seemed to fade out as Joe reflected on how he used to listen to those words so many times before, even hummed along, but never, had he applied them to himself . . . until now. Joe switched off the radio. "Amen," he whispered. *(Are You trying to tell me something, Lord? I messed things up quite a bit today, didn't I? I feel I'm failing everyone who has called on me. Am I failing You too? Maybe I'm not as solid as I like to think I am. Why did You pick me? What was it in me, that You felt would make a good priest?)* Joe thought of his own theme at his homily during that very morning. Only now he felt he should redirect the question: "What makes *me* so special?"

49

CHAPTER 3

BUT YOU DON'T KNOW ME

(Tuesday)

It can't be! How can anyone possibly be happy enough at 6:15 in the morning to sing in the shower? Joe thought as he turned on his side and tried to shut out George's rendition of "Raindrops Keep Falling on My Head." *(I wish he would lower his voice. Just when I can sleep an extra hour. It figures . . . just my luck he knows all the verses too.)* Finally, Joe heard the water shut off and George wind up with, "Nothin's worryin' me-e-e-e-e . . ." *(I'm happy for you. Now go away and say the seven o'clock Mass and let me get a few more winks.)*

Joe could hear George's shaver buzzing; he didn't seem to mind that because the hum was almost soothing. Suddenly he heard in a loud baritone, "You're just too good to be true. Can't take my eyes off of you. You'd be like heaven to . . ." *(God, no, a medley!)* Joe grinned at the image he had conjured up in his mind; George singing to himself in the mirror as he shaved. "At long last love has arrived and I thank God I'm alive. You're just too good to be true. Can't take my eyes off . . ." *(And I thank God I'm alive! Maybe that's George's way of saying his morning prayers.)* Joe turned to his other side. *(Wonder why he's so happy? I hate happy people in the morning.)* The clear tones of George's voice changed to a confusing muffled sound. *(I don't believe it! He even hums while he brushes his teeth!)* Finally the bathroom door shut and quiet prevailed once more. *(Lovely. Forty more minutes of sleep!)*

Joe had just about dozed off again when there was a gentle knocking at the door accompanied by a "loud" whisper, "Joe, you up? I have to ask you a favor."

"I am now. Come in; the door's not locked." Joe rolled on to his back and folded his arms behind his head.

George entered, wearing a pair of dark gray knit pants and a red turtle-neck sweater. "Can I borrow your cassock? Mine's in the cleaners and Monsignor Flannagan blows his mind when we walk over to say Mass in civvies. You don't mind, do you? I'll bring it back as soon as I finish Mass."

"No, go ahead. It's lying over the chair." Joe nodded toward the green leather chair in the corner of the room.

"Thanks." George reached for the cassock and began slipping it on. As he started buttoning the neck, he looked around Joe's room.

"Want something else?" Joe asked, waiting for his visitor to leave.

"No, I was just looking at how neat you keep your room. Mine's a mess."

"Oh," Joe said blankly. *(Who cares?)*

George started for the door. "Thanks again." He shut the door, then reopened it quickly. "Almost forgot. You going to the Ladies' Guild tonight?"

"I don't know. Why?"

"Monsignor wants me to run some slides and give a small talk about high-school catechetics, then have a discussion period. I'm not looking forward to it, frankly. The good ladies of St. Monica's and I don't speak the same language. I was kind of hoping you would be there — give me moral support, you know. If I ever really told them how I think religion should be taught in our high schools today, they'd have that phone ringing off the wall."

"Better go easy on them then," Joe advised.

"Yeah," George answered with a devilish grin. His blond hair was almost reaching his collar and his long sideburns framed his boyish smile. "Maybe I'll see you tonight. See ya." *(Might as well get up.)* Joe sat up on the side of the bed, rested his elbows on his knees and rubbed his eyes. When he stood, the hardwood floor sent a chill clear up his spine. Joe reached in his closet for his robe and headed for the shower.

"Good morning, Father," Dearie greeted as Joe entered the kitchen.

"Good morning," Joe answered as he muffled a yawn. "The Monsignor still taking his meals in his room?" Joe watched Mrs. Quinlan place a cup of warm milk and a bowl of hot cereal on a tray.

Dearie nodded. "Poor man's down to nothing. I'm worried about him, Father." Joe shook his head side to side sympathetically.

"And how are you today, Father?" Joe directed his attention to Father Benetti who was having his last cup of tea with the newspaper.

Father Benetti looked up but didn't answer the greeting. "Did you see this?" He pointed out the article about two priests running for political office up East, then shook his head. "You would think they had enough to do with their work in the Church. Where does it all end?"

"Imagine that . . ." Father Joe answered in a most complying voice. *(I bet if George were here, he would tell you what he thought.)*

"Did Father Pieri call for me last night while I was out, Dearie?" Joe asked as she reentered the kitchen. "No, Father . . . no calls at all. How's your brother?"

"Worried. Kate's pregnant again. That will give them five. Not bad for being married only five years, eh?"

"Poor thing," Dearie answered with a compassionate expression.

"God will bless them! They're fine Catholics," Father Benetti stated emphatically in his Italian accent, then left the room to read his office and listen to his records.

Suddenly the kitchen door swung open and George popped in; he seemed to be in a rush. "No breakfast for me today, Dearie. Want to get to the university early." He ran through the kitchen and down the hall towards his room. A few minutes later he emerged from his room wearing a yellow cardigan over the red turtle-neck sweater. "Got to run. Oh, Joe, your cassock's across my bed . . . forgot to put it in your room. Sorry."

"Honestly, that boy hardly ever eats breakfast. Where does he get his energy?" Dearie said as she cleared a few dishes from the table.

"He has what they call 'youth,' Dearie."

"He reminds me so much of my Johnny and the way he looked right after he was ordained . . . only twenty-five, he was, but he still looked like a young boy. So much energy. Johnny was always such a joy, Father Joe." Dearie lifted the corner of her apron and wiped her eyes.

This was a scene Joe had become quite accustomed to since he had first met Mrs. Quinlan: each time she spoke of her son she became misty. It had been almost five years now since she had last seen Johnny when he was missioned to Bolivia. The work there was quite uphill and from the looks of the few photographs John sent home, it was beginning to show a strain on him. Still with all his work, he was faithful in sending at least one letter a week to his mother.

"John may be coming home for a visit soon, with the help of God," Dearie said as her expression changed, showing a little excitement. "It would be nice if he would be home to celebrate his fortieth birthday. But I guess that's not important . . . just to see him for myself is all that matters."

Joe ran into George's room to reclaim his cassock. The huge brass peace symbol hanging from above the bed immediately roped Joe's attention; he had never seen anything so gigantic for such a small room. His eyes roamed around slowly. *(This is too much.)* In one corner there sat a record cabinet; George owned quite a collection, judging by the quantity of its contents. On a small desk there were two stacks of textbooks, a typewriter, and a small cassette tape recorder and a desk lamp from which was draped a set of love beads. The dresser was loaded with photographs. Joe's curiosity lured him closer to investigate them. The largest photo was of George's ordination group, with George standing right in the middle. He looked different in the photo: his hair was much shorter and his sideburns were not quite so long, a striking contrast to the smaller photo next to it. There

George was seated on the back of a small boat; he was clad in a pair of swimming trunks and a sweat shirt while he held a tackle line that displayed one small fish which appeared to be not more than three inches long. His hair was windblown and he appeared to be in need of a shave badly. The only other image on the photo was a girl, a very pretty girl, also in a bathing suit. The pair seemed to be laughing at George's big "catch." *(Maybe that's his sister? But she seems awfully dark to be related to George.)* Joe felt a little guilty as he explored the other possibilities in his mind; he felt as if he were invading George's privacy.

Another picture showed George standing between an elderly couple. *(I guess that's his mother and father. Certainly there's a resemblance there.)* There were several pictures of George with various groups of young men. *(Probably from his seminary days, I'll bet. Sure, it is. There's Bob Roth, the assistant at Holy Ghost parish . . . thought so.)* The last picture Joe studied carefully: it was one of a huge Christmas tree with George standing in the middle of the couple whom Joe had surmised were his parents in the previous photo. On each side of the parents stood two figures. Next to the mother were two girls who appeared to be in their late teens, and on the side of the father were two young men Joe judged to be in their early twenties. Everyone in the group was fair-haired and they all bore a family resemblance. *(Of course, a family picture . . . good one, too. But where's the brunette who was in the boat? Must not be his sister after all . . . a cousin, maybe?)*

Joe reached for his cassock as he glanced toward the chair next to the bed. There were a pair of khaki pants, a tie-dyed sweat shirt, and a lightweight beige jacket. On the floor lay a pair of sneakers and a pair of sand boots. Looks more like a college kid's room, Joe thought as he looked up at the walls. There was hardly a bare spot. Joe counted three huge gaudy banners. He read them with intrigue. "Smile, God Loves You"; "Today Is the First Day of the Rest of Your Life"; "Love Is a Helluva Lot of Work!" *(Wild . . . I've been living across the hall from this guy for almost a year and I've never really seen the inside of his room before. Really never had the occasion to.)* Joe realized how little he really knew about his associate. *(George*

54

was right about one thing — his room really is a big mess!)

At Mass, Joe prayed hard for his brother Tim, and Kate. He asked God to help them through their present dilemma and to give them the strength to accept the little soul He had entrusted to them. Then he prayed for guidance for Ed Pieri to sift out his problems and return to his apostolate. *(And don't forget Gregg Bruno and Pam Davis. Both of them are mixed up and they need You at this time during their lives. I had the chance to make them aware of how much they needed You, but I muffed it. You know how much I need You to tell me the right things to say. I know what I should say, but half the time I get carried away with my own impatience and temper. I work on it, but it doesn't seem to get any better. Give me patience, Lord. And please help me to help those who come to me with their troubles. I'm not very good at it, Lord . . . I still can't understand why You picked me.)*

When Mass was finished, Joe started across the church parking lot toward the rectory; he quickened his pace when he spied Ed's car in the driveway.

"Where is he?" Joe asked Mrs. Quinlan anxiously as he opened the kitchen door.

"Father Pieri's in Father Benetti's room. He's been here since right after you left for Mass."

"What's he doing in there?" Joe mumbled as he headed down the hall; he could hear soft strains of an operatic overture as he approached Father Benetti's room. The door was slightly ajar; Joe could see Father Benetti sitting in his huge old rocker, waving his arms as if he were the conductor of a large symphony orchestra. His eyes were closed as though he was shutting out the rest of the world, leaving him to absorb nothing but the music that now featured the woodwind section. Joe pushed the door open wider. There was Ed straddling the desk chair as he rested his elbows on the backrest. Ed nodded to Joe, then put his index finger to his lips in a motion "to be quiet." Joe stood there motionless for a moment until the tune ended with a quiet fading of the string section, as Father Benetti rested his hands on his lap and opened his eyes. The old man began to rattle off a mile a minute in Italian to Ed; Ed answered in the same tongue.

The dialogue continued for several minutes until Ed pointed to Joe and both Italian priests began to laugh heartily.

"I have the feeling you're talking about me," Joe said, smiling. He was glad to see Ed in such good spirits. *(His visit with Schumacher must have done him some good.)*

Ed rose from his chair and slid it back to its proper place behind the desk. In Italian again, he thanked the old priest for the pleasure of his company, and his records. Father Benetti rose and hugged Ed in the manner of Latins. Turning to Joe, he said, "Your friend is a good priest . . . and a good Italian. He appreciates beautiful music!"

Joe mumbled something in agreement, then motioned to Ed to follow him to the parlor; he couldn't wait to talk to him alone.

"Well?"

"Well, what?" Ed answered, lighting a cigarette and taking a chair.

"Did you see Schumacher?"

"I went," was Ed's terse reply.

"So?" Joe asked impatiently.

"So what?" Ed grinned; he was deliberately trying to annoy Joe. He knew his friend's impatience.

Joe threw his arms in the air. "You're *something else!*"

"Don't get nervous," Ed said, smiling. "Yes, I did talk to Schumacher. Yes, I am going to take his advice and go to the retreat house for a couple of days. Yes, he did help me. Yes, I talked to the old man and cleared it to get away for a while, and yes, I'm heading for the retreat house as soon as I leave here. Now, that should answer all your questions. Sit down, I have a favor to ask of you."

"Anything. Shoot."

"I know you always have dinner at your mother's on Wednesday nights. Whatever you do, don't talk to her about my plans, will you? I mean what I said about leaving the priesthood. You know how your mother and mine get on the phone and gab and I wouldn't want to have anything slip out inadvertently. I haven't talked to either of my parents about this yet — not till I'm sure; and you know how upset they would be." *("Not till I'm sure. . . ." That sounds good. Yesterday he said his mind was made up. Schumacher must have really started him thinking.)*

Ed continued, "My sister knows, but I can depend on her to keep quiet."

"Don't worry. I hadn't even considered mentioning it to anybody. Is there anything else?"

"Yeah . . . why don't you spend a few minutes once in a while with that old guy in there? He was like a little kid because he had someone to listen to the music with him. He's lonely, Joe. That old guy is really lonely . . ."

Joe walked Ed to the door, assured him he would remember him at Mass, then started for Benetti's room when Dearie stopped him.

"Monsignor Flannagan wants to see you, Father Joe."

"Be right there, Dearie," Joe answered as he knocked on the old priest's door. Father Benetti yelled, "Come in," as he turned the volume lower on his record player.

"I just wanted to tell you, Father . . ." Joe stammered. *(Tell him what? I seldom say much of anything to him unless it pertains to the Mass schedule or the weather.)*

"Yes, Father?" Benetti asked, waiting.

"I just wanted to tell you how much I enjoy your music . . . every once in a while I can hear it softly coming from your room. It's very nice."

Joe emerged a few minutes later carrying a small stack of records which Father Benetti guaranteed would be both enjoyable and relaxing. He even offered Joe a sample of a special blend of tobacco a relative sent to him periodically from the old country and invited Joe to listen to his music with him anytime he wished. Joe thanked him and went to put the records in his room. *(That's strange . . . I never thought of Benetti as being lonely before. Ed saw something in the old man I have never seen in all the time I've lived here. Ed saw it; why didn't I? But then Benetti and I are worlds apart . . . George and I are too, come to think of it.)*

"You wanted to see me, Monsignor?" Joe asked as he entered the pastor's office.

"Sit down, Joe. I have a couple of things to run over with you. I'm depending on you to carry the load around here till this

57

belly of mine quits acting up." The pastor's complexion was almost ashen. It was obvious he was losing weight much too rapidly; even his stiff Roman collar seemed to almost drape around his neck. Joe had never remembered seeing the monsignor look so listless.

The elder priest leaned back in his chair to light his pipe.

"You're not supposed to be smoking, are you?"

"Not really," Monsignor Flannagan dismissed his disobedience with a tremendous puff of smoke. "Tonight's the Ladies' Guild and I asked George to show some slides and prepare a little talk. Figured maybe it would give him a chance to gain a little interest in some of the parish activities. And the subject matter was something familiar to him, teaching in the high school and all."

"He mentioned it," Joe volunteered.

The pastor nodded. "I'd like you to be there too, Joe. Kind of look over things in case George locks horns with some of our conservatives during the discussion period. Don't want him to 'lose his cool' as you young people put it. Can I count on you?"

Joe shook his head affirmatively.

"Another thing . . . I hate to make a public relations man out of you." The pastor paused pensively, then continued, "But you know a parish priest spends a great deal of his time doing just that." Flannagan said as almost an afterthought, "I want you to keep the lines open between the rectory and the faculty at the school. Sister Jeanine has been a little uneasy the past few days about the behavior in the school yard and some of the lay teachers' absenteeism. Keep her happy. She's made a lot of concessions in the past and one good turn deserves another . . . know what I mean?"

"I understand."

"You know St. Monica's is lucky to have such an outstanding teaching order as our nuns. They've kept the caliber of lay teachers high too. They've even compromised with me and stayed in a semi-conservative habit while most of the others in their community have gone totally to lay dress. St. Monica's, being basically conservative, I think that makes our parishioners happy — and me too!" The pastor grinned. "I'm going to make up a list of a few things that will need attention and maybe you could —" Flannagan grimaced, grabbed his stomach and leaned forward with a slight moan.

"Are you all right?" Joe asked, rising from his chair.

"Lousy ulcer." Flannagan strained, then took a deep breath as if he were trying to regain control. "As I was saying, if you could — " He stopped again and began to take deep labored breaths. Joe grabbed the monsignor's shoulders to guide him against the back rest of the chair.

"Is there anything I can do?" Joe asked helplessly. Flannagan shook his head negatively. "I have an appointment with Nowaski this morning..."

"I'll drive you," Joe said as he left the room to get his jacket.

"Dearie, call the school and tell Sister Jeanine that I'm not taking my classes this morning," Joe ordered excitedly. "I'm taking Monsignor to the doctor's. Be back later."

"Is the monsignor worse?" Dearie questioned as she followed Joe down the hall.

"Don't know, but he doesn't look so hot. Don't forget to call Sister Jeanine."

The waiting room was almost filled when Joe and Monsignor Flannagan arrived at Doctor Nowaski's. Joe found two unoccupied seats together and motioned to his pastor to sit. They were just about to take their chairs when the nurse emerged from the anteroom of the office and announced that the monsignor could go right in. A half hour later she reappeared and requested that Joe see Doctor Nowaski in his office.

"Your boss is getting dressed. Take a seat," Doctor Nowaski said as he switched on the lights of the X-ray bar. "See this?" He slid an X-ray into the small slot at the top of the lights. "Doesn't look good, does it?"

Joe remained silent, staring at the picture. He didn't know what it looked like. All he could make out was a complete set of ribs on one side; but on the other side only a couple of ribs were discernible — the rest were blurred. "What does it mean?"

"It means the mad Irishman's leaving here and going straight to Mercy Hospital. My orders. This is one time that thick head is not going to talk me out of it! And that's that!"

Doctor Nowaski and Monsignor Flannagan were more than just friends — they were "family." Theirs was a friendship that began in their boyhood days and had waxed with each passing year. They seemed to take great pride in affectionately insulting each other.

"He's not too good then?" Joe asked stupidly.

"No, he's not 'too good.' Fact is, he's damn sick. Get him in there right away. I already called the hospital and ordered him a bed. I'm running some tests this afternoon so I can give you a better picture tomorrow, if you want to call me then." Doctor Nowaski swiveled his chair facing the X-ray as he squinted his eyes. "For now, let's just say you guys better get to work on the Man upstairs!"

"Are you comfortable, Father?" Joe asked as he slipped behind the steering wheel and turned on the ignition.

"I'm all right. Take me back to the rectory."

"They're waiting for you at Mercy. Doctor Nowaski gave me strict orders to — "

"Never mind," the monsignor interrupted. "You take your orders from me, not Nowaski . . . and I'm telling you to take me back to the rectory. I'm going to pack my pajamas before I go. I'm not going to give that old Polack the satisfaction of having some nurse slap any hospital gown on me!"

Joe sat in a chair outside the admitting office waiting for Monsignor Flannagan to finish filling out all the necessary forms. (I hate hospitals . . . they smell. Always remind me of when I was a kid and had to go to the dentist's . . . hated the smell there too.) Joe reached for a magazine and began to page through it. One story, accompanied by a photo, caught his eye. It pictured a small group of casually dressed young men and women sitting in a very informal atmosphere; the caption read, "Seated from left to right are: the former priest, Father _____; the former nun, Sister _____; Father _____, etc." The main topic was the changing Church, but celibacy seemed to take up the greatest amount of copy. There were several statistics given from polls taken from present clerics and religious regarding their opinions on this subject. *(How come nobody ever asks me? Every time I pick up one of these things they quote hundreds of priests who were asked various questions to arrive at a total for these polls, but I don't know one of us guys who was ever asked.)*

The article clearly stated that those in the picture who had been interviewed all agreed that the Church wasn't relevant to today's needs and that since they have left their former professions and were working outside the Church structure, they could relate better to their fellowman. *(Big deal! So they can all relate to each other. Who cares? The Church is better off without them . . . but then, who am I to judge? How many times have I felt like throwing in the towel? If they want to leave, that's their business; but why do they always have to start knocking us suckers who are trying to make it? That's the part that bugs me most: right away they want to make everybody feel the same way they do . . .)*

Joe's thoughts were interrupted when he became conscious of the middle-aged woman sitting next to him, practically reading over his shoulder. *(I'll bet she's wondering what my reaction is to this.)* Joe moved uncomfortably in his chair, then turned the page. *(That will take care of her!)* The article on the next page was entitled, and in bold print, "Sex After Menopause." Joe quickly turned the page again!

By the time Joe waited for the monsignor to get settled in his room and returned to the rectory, it was close to two. The antiseptic smell from the hospital had robbed Joe of an appetite although it was well past lunch and he had eaten nothing since breakfast. He returned his mother's call, promised he would be there by five for dinner the next day, and assured her that he didn't have a cold — just a touch of sinus congestion and that there was nothing to worry about. There was no sense in going to the school since classes were about finished for the day, so he decided to go to his room and recapture that extra hour's sleep George had interrupted that morning. Joe wasn't too certain that he could sleep, but he could at least get a little rest.

"Father Joe, dinner's ready ... Father Joe?" *(Dinner!)* Joe looked at his watch; it was 5:30. *(Can't be. I just dozed off for a minute. Well, it felt like a minute!)*

Joe explained to George and Father Benetti about the pastor's admittance to Mercy at dinner. He omitted the information about the pessimism that Doctor Nowaski displayed regarding Monsignor Flannagan's condition. He felt there was no need to alarm them further until he talked with Nowaski tomorrow. George and Joe discussed that evening's Ladies' Guild meeting while Benetti merely listened in.

Joe was about to sit down for the evening news when the telephone rang. "It's for you, Father Joe," Dearie called.

"Father Newman speaking." It was Joe's professional voice.

"Hi, Father. It's me, Gregg Bruno. Remember?"

"Gregg! How did you know how to reach me?"

"Called the chancery and they gave me your number." There was a long pause. "Hey, listen ... the reason I called was to apologize to you about the other night. I guess I acted like a jerk, running off like that." His voice projected a great deal of embarrassment.

"Forget it. You had a lot on your mind to be uptight about," Joe comforted. "How's things going?" Joe was trying to sound casual although his mind was racing with a thousand ways to try to approach the boy again.

"Okay, I guess. Maybe I'll give you a call sometime soon and we'll have that talk?"

"You know where to reach me," Joe offered.

"Yeah. . . . Thanks. I'll give you a call . . . I mean it, Father. Okay?"

"Anytime, Gregg . . . and thanks for calling."

"Bye." The phone clicked on the other end. Joe sat there for a few seconds still holding the phone. *(Maybe I didn't lose this one after all? Giving me a second chance, Lord?)*

After the slides were shown, George created the scene for discussion by opening with, "Any comments or questions?" The first hand to rise belonged to Mrs. Ferris.

"All these new approaches to teaching religion sound great in theory, but I don't see any results. If they are supposed to be so good, why doesn't it show in our young people? I see very few Christian attitudes formed in them. All you ever hear about is drugs and sex, drugs and sex. And our Catholic kids, I daresay, are involved in it just as much as anyone else. We should bring back the old Baltimore catechism . . . that *did* get results! If you ask me — " She couldn't finish because of the applause.

"Who asked her?" George whispered to Joe under his breath as he rose to answer.

"Mrs. Ferris, the whole reason for all these slides was to show new ways to teach our teen-agers in a way that they will respond to. Our approach must be different in order to meet their needs. What may have been effective yesterday, may not be tomorrow. Times change — "

"But morals do not!" Mrs. Ferris broke in heatedly. Nods of agreement from a few ladies around her gave her more encouragement. "And how can we expect our kids to learn right from wrong if some of our priests don't even know!" Once again, the hall vibrated with more applause.

"But who are *you* to make that judgment?" George accused.

"I know this, Father Rahner. Some priests are certainly no example to our young people when they try to look and dress just like one of them." Mrs. Ferris focused her gaze on George's long hair and George was aware of it. "You can't blame the young people for acting and dressing the way they do when — "

"No, you can't blame them!" George interrupted. "You can't blame them at all for rebelling against a society that places too much emphasis on what you wear or how long your hair is, when those same people don't take the time to look at what's inside."

There was a buzz among the audience. Joe didn't know if the reaction was due to what George said or the way he said it. Before Mrs. Ferris could offer a rebuttal, Joe pounded the gavel and in a very calm voice, he said, "I think we're off the issue. We're here to discuss catechetics in our high schools, not dress. I would like to comment on some of the new methods shown in the slides we've seen this evening. It seems to me that all of us are interested in the same goal, to give our Catholic youth sound

Christian teachings, then show them how to incorporate them in their everyday living. The method is simply a tool to attain the end results. As religious educators, we must seek methods which bring the best results, *then* make use of them." There was a small round of applause and nods of approval. Joe felt it was best to quit while he was ahead and let a few tempers cool down. "Now let's stop for a break and we'll continue after the refreshments are served."

As the crowd began to gather at the coffee bar and the women took up their chatter, Joe turned to George and whispered, "Try not to look so uptight. You want some coffee?"

"No. Listen, Joe, how about you taking over from here? This just isn't my bag. She was getting at me, Joe. You saw it!"

"Look, you're just getting your feet wet. Don't give up so easily. It happens to all of us. Stay."

"No, thanks. They don't even try to see things as they really are. If I have to go through all the motions that you just did to pacify them, I'd be as phony as they are. I'm cutting out. See you later at the rectory."

The rest of the meeting went smoothly as Joe put on the charm, trying to pretend that the previous incident didn't even happen. Before the meeting closed, Joe explained that Father Rahner had been called away, but that he wished to express the parish's thanks to him for preparing the slides and presenting them so well. Several women complimented Joe on his tact at handling what could have become a real confrontation. Joe accepted the compliments, but throughout it all, he felt an uneasiness. *(Was George inferring that I was a phony too? But I was just doing my job. That's what Monsignor Flannagan said this morning. "Public relations" he called it . . .)*

George was seated alone in the den when Joe returned to the rectory. "Want that cup of coffee now?" Joe asked.

George followed him into the kitchen and put two cups at the table while Joe started filling the electric percolator. "I envy you, Joe."

"Why?"

"You always know what to say at the right time. You're smooth. Know what I mean?"

"If you're referring to what happened tonight at the meeting, well — "

"Not just that . . . all the time. You're really cut out for all of this. What I mean is, you don't have any hang-ups, do you?"

"Hang-ups about what?" Joe asked, puzzled.

"About being a priest. It all comes easy to you."

"I have doubts and problems just like you or anybody else, but — "

"Not big ones, though," George interrupted. "There's no 'Punch or Judy' with you."

Joe was surprised to hear the young priest use an expression that was familiar to the older clergy.

"You mean 'booze or women'? No, I don't have any 'real' problems there, but I still have problems. I'm always wondering if I'm doing a good job or not."

"That's it! You're wondering *how* you're doing the job . . . I wonder if I'm *doing* a job at all. You follow me?"

Joe waited for an explanation; the conversation wasn't clear to him.

"You see, with me I'm not too sure. Like I feel I have to be me before I can be anything else. I need people too. I can't fit in that little priestly mold that makes a priest detached, different from everybody else. For one thing . . . I like women." The last statement threw Joe; he wasn't too sure where it was leading. "Do you like women, Joe?"

"Of course, I have to deal with them all the time, counseling, and —"

George interrupted, looking at Joe closely: "Do you know any women? I mean really 'know' them? How many friends do you have that are women?"

Joe felt as if he were being cross-examined. "How do you mean?"

"Let me put it this way. Could you just pick up the phone and call a female friend just to gab or spend an evening with her exchanging ideas?"

Joe stared at the coffee cup as he probed George's speculation. The situation that George illustrated was a luxury Joe had never permitted. The consequence of such an act could lead to a more intimate involvement. He looked up at George. "For the sake of prudence, I — "

" 'Would not'! Right? Because you're afraid of getting involved. Don't you see? That's what I'm getting at. A priest just shouldn't do something like that. We're supposed to have all the right answers for all human experiences without ever experiencing ourselves. How can we experience anything if we're keeping a clerical harness around our emotions all the time, staying detached, not getting involved, or whatever you want to call it?"

Joe said nothing. This wasn't a new argument; he had heard it all before from dozens of other people, but it was something Joe couldn't really argue. *(Maybe George is right. I don't have any real hang-ups, but that doesn't mean I don't feel things.)*

Joe tried to explain. "I can sympathize with everything you're saying, George. I really can. But as a priest, I must put restrictions on my actions in order to keep order in my way of life. The example you gave about calling a lady friend . . . okay, let's talk about it." Joe pushed his coffee cup away to give him more room to illustrate his point with hand gestures. "I do like women. As a man, I want what they can offer me: friendship, warmth, affection, whatever. But as a priest, I have to accept from them only those things that my total commitment to the priesthood will allow. The temptations are great enough when we're talking about simple biology. I'm not too certain I could weather them if there were a close involvement too. In other words, why stand inside a bakery looking at all the goodies if you're not allowed to eat them? You're better off not going in."

"That's what I mean when I said you're lucky . . . no hang-ups. I envy you." George sipped his coffee. His serious mood was foreign to Joe.

"Maybe you just have 'growing pains,' " Joe teased as he stirred his coffee. "But that's good. If you don't experience them, how are you going to 'grow'?"

When Joe went to the sink to leave his cup, he noticed a light shining from the church. Suddenly it dawned on him that he had forgotten to turn out the light in the sacristy when he had been there earlier to give one of the ladies the altar linens to launder. "I'm running over to the church a minute, George. Be right

66

back." George grunted something which sounded like, "Take your time. I'm not going anywhere."

There's nothing more quiet or spooky than a deserted church at night, Joe thought. His footsteps echoed through the structure as he walked down the long aisle. He rested his eyes on the huge crucifix suspended over the main altar. A shaft of light from the sacristy caught the figure of the crucified Christ, creating an impression Joe had never noticed before. The face of Christ was beautiful but sad. Beads of blood streamed from the skull torn by thorns which encircled the temples and forehead; the eyes seemed to be pleading. Tears welled in the swollen eyelids. Every muscle and vein in the face and body was strained. The artist has really captured the suffering Christ, Joe thought. He turned to switch off the light in the sacristy and walked back toward the center of the altar. He genuflected before the tabernacle of the Blessed Sacrament, then looked at the face once again. It was still aglow from the sanctuary lamp casting its amber reflection. Joe knelt in the darkness. *(Just You and me now, Lord. No need for me to look for the right words or the right way to say them. You know what's on my mind. I feel pride when people tell me I'm a good priest, but after my argument with George, I feel ashamed. Am I putting up a big front? George thinks I'm a good priest; so do a lot of other people . . . I guess. Only You know what goes on here inside. Who am I selling? You, or Father Joe Newman — super priest? I don't always know the answers to that one. I gave George all the right answers . . . I think. And I gave him the impression that I had no hang-ups about how to be a good priest. But he doesn't really know me. Nobody knows what another's really like . . . only You know that. You know all our weaknesses and frustrations . . . and still You permit us to share in Your priesthood. In spite of all our failings and faults, Your word somehow gets through to those who are looking for You.)*

CHAPTER 4

MATTER OF LIFE AND DEATH
(Wednesday)

It took some time for the incessant sound of the ringing of the telephone to penetrate Joe's brain and bring him back to consciousness. He sat up abruptly, shook his head and groped for the switch on the bed lamp. His clock told him it was 4 a.m. *(Who could be calling at this hour of the morning?)* He grabbed his robe and made his way to the door. Still half-asleep, he picked up the telephone. "St. Monica's. Father Newman here."

"This is Memorial Hospital, Father," a woman's voice responded. "We need a priest. It's an emergency. The patient is not expected to live. Can you get here right away? The patient's name is Tom Baxter."

The word "emergency" brought Joe to full consciousness. "I'll be there in ten minutes!" he said, then banged the phone on the receiver and rushed to his room.

Within three minutes, he was running across the church parking lot on his way to pick up the Blessed Sacrament. Ten minutes later, he walked in the emergency entrance of the hospital.

"Where will I find Tom Baxter?" Joe asked the nurse at the desk.

"He's in the emergency room across the hall, Father. They're waiting for you."

Joe met the doctor at the doorway. "You're just about in time, Father. He's barely conscious. I don't think he'll last much longer. There's nothing more we can do for him. It was a car wreck. When are these kids going to learn that cars and pot don't mix? A damn waste . . . that's what it is, a damn waste." The doctor shook his head disgustedly as he walked away.

Joe entered the room and cast his eyes on the battered body; the stench of blood and burnt flesh overwhelmed the antiseptic smell, and Joe felt sick; his legs began to tremble. The boy's face was invisible from the angle Joe was looking. As he approached the hospital cart, he wanted to turn away. The boy's arm was exposed; the flesh was hardly recognizable as human. Joe's attention was diverted momentarily by the sobbing of the boy's parents. Soon he was standing over the cart looking down into the boy's face; it was unmarked except for a small cut above the eye.

The nurse ushered the wet-eyed parents out of the room while the father held his wife tightly and tried to lead her away. "Tommy, Tommy," she cried desperately.

Joe placed his stole over his shoulders and leaned over the dying boy. "Tom, I'm a priest. Can you hear me?"

The young boy opened his eyes. His breathing was deep and labored. He could only nod. Joe laid his hand on the boy's head. "Don't try to speak. I'll hear your confession . . . just nod if the answer is 'yes.' " Joe began questioning him about his probable sins and received confirmation or denial by an appropriate nod. "Are you sorry for all your sins, Tom?" Joe whispered.

The boy's lips were straining to move, tears began to fill his shocked eyes. "S-s-s-s-s-scared, F-f-father . . . s-s-s-s-scared . . ."

"Don't be frightened, Tom. Believe that God loves you and wants you."

"Stay . . . stay," Tom murmured.

"I'll be right here beside you. I won't leave. God is here too. He'll use my hands to anoint you. Don't be frightened. God is with you." Joe removed the holy oils and began anointing. "By this holy anointing, may you be forgiven of all your sins against sight . . ." Joe touched Tom's eyes with his anointed finger and thumb; he felt the hot tears. He then moved to the nose, and to the ears. When he reached the mouth, the boy's lips were trembling and cold. Joe's anointed fingers moved over Tom's exposed

69

hands: he shuddered as he felt the burnt flesh through the holy oils. He lifted the sheet to anoint the other hand, the skin was gone. When he exposed Tom's feet, the stench of burnt flesh grew stronger. The short glimpse of the torn body staggered Joe for a second. He closed his eyes and tried desperately to concentrate on every word as he completed the anointing. He raised his hand in absolution, then leaned down over the boy's face once again. After he placed the Sacred Host on Tom's tongue, he leaned back and rested his hand on the side of the cart. His fingers touched the boy's. He felt the boy's hand clasp his own.

"Stay . . . please . . . stay," came the moans from the boy's throat.

"I won't leave, Tom. Hold my hand. Think of Christ. We'll pray together." Joe knelt beside the cart, then motioned for the parents to reenter the room. They knelt at the other side of the cart as Joe continued the prayers and Scriptures from the ritual. The only sound other than his own voice was the quiet sobbing from the boy's parents. As he completed the readings, Tom's breathing became louder; he was gasping. Suddenly with unbelievable strength, he called out, "Mom . . . Mom . . . Dad . . ." His chest rose and he choked out his last breath.

Joe bowed his head and begged God to welcome the youth. The realization of what had just happened hit the boy's mother and she stood sobbing uncontrollably. "Tommy! Tommy!" she screamed. Her husband held her tightly once again; he couldn't speak and tears were streaming from his eyes. They held onto each other and looked at their dead son. The doctor and nurse went toward them while Joe rushed out of the room. The couple followed.

Joe had completed the easiest part of his priestly duties; the divine nature of his priesthood had performed its work, but now as he faced the dead boy's parents, he was completely aware of his own human nature and its inadequacy. The boy's mother clasped his hand, "Why, Father? He was only seventeen. Why my boy?" she cried.

Joe swallowed deeply and gave out all the pious platitudes he had learned so well. He was, this minute, the perfect priest — strong, compassionate and full of words of wisdom and consolation. How well he could play his part, but he was trained well. They thanked him, then he excused himself, promising to return in a moment. He went to the lavatory where he felt he could be alone. The horror of the dead boy and the misery of his heartbroken family conquered, and Joe — safe, now that he was alone — leaned against the washbasin, weeping. He found himself asking the same question the mother asked, "Why? Why, God? He was so young . . ."

When he entered the hall again, he paid his respects once again to the grief-stricken couple, then turned to leave. When he passed the doorway of the emergency room, he saw the lifeless body still lying there. Now, the face was covered. The sickening stench of the burnt flesh and blood pierced his senses and he staggered momentarily. He quickened his pace to almost a run and found his way to his car. He leaned against the hood for a second, realizing coldly the human nature of his priesthood. He could feel the rotted flesh in his anointed fingers and the horrible stench wouldn't leave his senses. He vomited.

It was 8:05 when Joe walked into the sacristy to vest for Mass. If Mrs. Quinlan hadn't wakened him, he would have been even later for Mass. It was past five when Joe arrived back at the rectory and way past six when he finally dozed off, after spending a good fifteen minutes in the shower. He wanted to get rid of the deathly stench that seemed to cling to his very person. If only he could wash this from his mind as well as from his body, he thought, as he remained under the warm spray. Now, as he vested, he felt exhausted, yet tense. He was glad this was his day off.

"Get the hymn numbers from Sister Margaret, Bill. Tony, you bring the cross. Let's go . . . we're late!" he said as he placed the alb over his head and reached for the cincture. Joe was still dazed from his interrupted sleep as he followed the altar boys up the aisle. He looked up at the face of the crucified Christ just as he had done the night before; the daylight seemed to accent His suffering even more than Joe remembered, or was it that he could see Tom's face there too? *(Tom certainly wasn't plaster. He was real; he was alive; he was suffering too, but now he was dead . . . and I watched him die.)* Mechanically he genuflected as he made his way to the chair. "In the name of the Father, and of the Son and of the Holy Spirit." Suddenly he realized he hadn't read the day's Gospel and he hadn't a clue as to what was to be his theme for the Mass. He paused. The picture of Tom's sobbing mother flashed before his eyes. How he wanted to console her, to tell her that death was the beginning of another life! The words came and Joe said loudly, "The theme of the Mass is 'Eternal life.' "

The first reading fitted the theme, he thought as he listened with more attention than usual to the words of St. Paul: "It is not I that live now, but Christ who lives in me . . ." The congregation joined in a moment of silent prayer while Joe quickly outlined his homily. As he moved toward the pulpit the fifth grade vigorously sang the "Alleluia." They seemed to be stronger and more prayerful than most days, but this particular class always put everything into the Mass; Joe found this to be true of these children in their religion classes too. He began to read the Gospel; it was uncanny. The Gospel was tailor-made for his theme and his thoughts. "My flesh is meat indeed. My blood is drink indeed. He that eats my body and drinks my blood will live forever . . ." Joe was moved by the aptness of the readings and mentally thanked the Holy Spirit for helping him once again. He had a story to tell the kids, Tom Baxter's. Now he had the right Scriptures to make sense of it; all he needed was to convince himself.

Later at the consecration of the Mass, Joe took the Host in his hands; he always found it difficult to believe it was his hands that were holding it. "This is my body which will be given up for you." He raised it above his head and held it there. This was the bread of eternal life! The bell was ringing. Again the body of Tom flashed through his mind and almost immediately he visualized the suffering, bleeding Christ in his prayers the night before. He took the cup, and thought of Tom's blood spilled last night. "This is the cup of my blood, the blood of the new and everlasting covenant; it will be shed for you and for all men for the forgiveness of sins." *("The forgiveness of sins . . .")* He had forgiven Tom's sins. Tom had entered into eternal life! Joe felt like a priest again. It was a feeling he could not adequately describe.

"You look tired, Father. I know you didn't get much sleep. I heard you leave after the phone rang and you were still shuffling around when I got up this morning to make sure Father Benetti would be on time for the six o'clock Mass," said Mrs. Quinlan as she put a cup of coffee before him. "Your eggs will be done in a minute."

"I am tired, Dearie," Joe said pensively.

"Today's your day off. Why don't you take a nap after you finish breakfast? Leave the phone calls to me."

"Thanks. I think I will, but if there are any calls you feel are important, wake me."

Just as Mrs. Quinlan put down the plate, the telephone rang. She rushed to answer it. "Mercy Hospital? Yes, he's here, but he's having breakfast at the moment — "

"It's okay. I'll take it," Joe interrupted.

"This is Father Newman. Yes, Doctor . . . I see . . ." There was a long pause as Mrs. Quinlan looked on anxiously. "Yes, I'll meet you in the doctors' lounge in about an hour . . . and thank you. Good-bye."

"Something's happened to the monsignor! I just know it," Mrs. Quinlan said nervously.

"Calm down, Dearie, we don't know that yet. That was Doctor Nowaski. He wants me to meet him. I couldn't understand all of that medical jargon but from what I gather, Monsignor went to surgery at seven this morning. He's in the recovery room now, but the doctor said he won't be back in his room for an hour or so. Doctor Nowaski wants to talk to me before I see Monsignor. I wonder why they didn't let us know he was getting operated on. They made no mention of it yesterday when I brought him there."

Joe entered the hospital and inquired where he could find the doctors' lounge. As he walked down the long hall, he was careful not to let his eyes wander to any of the open doors along the walls; he didn't want to see anything that would remind him of the latest scene he had visiting a hospital. Finally, he found the lounge and entered. There sitting in an easy chair writing something in a small black book was the doctor. He looked tired too. He was a small, thin man, almost bald. Joe knew the minute Doctor Nowaski raised his head that something was wrong.

"Hello, Father, sit down," he said, not rising from his chair.

"You said you wanted to talk with me before I see the monsignor — "

"Yes, and I'm not going to beat around the bush," the doctor interrupted. "We ran a few tests on Bill . . . Monsignor . . . yesterday. I told them to rush the results to me. As soon as I saw the X-rays and the blood tests that showed evidence of internal bleeding, I knew we were in big trouble so I scheduled him for surgery at seven this morning. Your boss has a thick head, as I guess you know, and he wouldn't let me notify anyone that he was going up. So I went along with him, but now I feel I had to call you. When we got him on the table and opened him up, there was nothing we could do but close. In other words, he's too far gone."

There was a short silence until Joe got over the initial shock well enough to speak. "Does he know?"

"Not yet. But he'll be in his room shortly. I expect he'll be able to talk before too long. We didn't have to use much anesthesia. Didn't really need to keep him out that long. Today's not the time to tell him." The doctor lit his pipe and drew in slowly, then rested back in the easy chair. "Bill's relatives are all gone. His only sister went just a few months back. There are no living relatives to contact, but Bill told me to keep in touch with you."

"Are you going to tell him, Doctor?"

Doctor Nowaski didn't evade Joe's question; rather he seemed to be thinking aloud. "You know, Bill and I grew up together and stayed friends all these years. Bill married us and baptized all my kids . . . even married a couple of them too. One thing, we've always been honest with one another. I'm not going to change that now. He's a priest, a thickheaded one, and he should know; but today's not the day . . . maybe tomorrow . . ."

Joe waited outside Monsignor Flannagan's room till the nurse gave him the okay to enter. The monsignor was quite alert, more so than Joe had expected. He crept into the room.

"Joseph . . . what are you doing here!" the pastor asked softly.

"I came to see you, but I didn't know you were getting operated on until just a little while ago. How are you feeling?" Joe asked nervously.

"They kind of cut me up a little, huh?" was the monsignor's delayed reply.

Joe didn't know what to say; he couldn't very well tell him he would be all better now, when in fact, his suffering was just beginning. And he certainly couldn't give any false hope when he knew there was none. "Try and sleep, Monsignor. I'll sit here with you if you like."

The elder priest nodded, and for a minute it looked as if he might be drifting off to sleep. With his eyes still closed, he said slowly, "Joe, tell Stanley that he's a good man and a good doctor, for a Polack." He smiled drowsily.

Joe was certain he didn't know what he was saying, that he was still under the effects of the anesthetic. "Where is the old crab? Did my good doctor desert me already?"

"He's coming up right away. He had to take a call," Joe answered, still not too sure that the monsignor was aware.

"Then you talked with him today?" The pastor's speech was very clear now; he seemed to show a little anxiety.

"Just for a minute. I ran into him on my way up here." Joe didn't want to show any alarm.

"Joe?"

"Yes, Monsignor?" Joe leaned toward him.

"It's not good, is it?" the pastor's eyes were searching, then he turned his gaze toward the ceiling. "You don't have to answer —"

"You're not supposed to be talking," Joe broke in; "try to sleep." He was trying to keep a casual voice, but he doubted if he was succeeding.

"I am tired . . . I'll try to sleep a while. You run along now." The monsignor moved his head to find a more comfortable position. Joe rose to leave. "Give me your blessing before you go, Joe."

Joe raised his hand for the blessing and the elder priest

made the sign of the cross weakly. When he finished, he took Joe's hand. "Sorry I put you on the spot . . . I already knew."

It was almost eleven when Mrs. Quinlan met Joe at the rectory door with a thousand questions about Monsignor Flannagan's condition. Joe told her that the pastor was resting comfortably and didn't seem to be in much pain. He hoped that answer would calm her for the time being. "Thank God," she said, blessing herself, then quickly went into a rundown of all the calls. "The phone's been going nonstop. The chancery called twice, the vicar-general wants you to call him as soon as you get in. There were eight calls for Monsignor. Most of them didn't leave their number. I expect those were the 'gossip' calls," she said with a snort of disgust. "And let me see, who else called? Oh, Father Wilson! He wants you to call right away too."

Joe went to the telephone while Dearie followed, still rattling on. "What do you think the vicar-general wanted? It's usually important when you hear from him. I hope there's no trouble —"

"Don't worry, Dearie. He may just want to know about Monsignor Flannagan's condition." Joe held a finger to his lips to quiet Mrs. Quinlan when he heard an answer to his call.

"Yes, Monsignor . . . the bishop wants to see me Friday at noon? I'll be there . . . thank you. Good-bye."

"My lands! The bishop wants to see you? Don't tell me they've taken their gossip to the bishop!" Dearie put her hand over her mouth as if she had let something slip out.

"What gossip, Dearie?"

"Father Joe . . . it's nothing, really. I shouldn't have said that." Mrs. Quinlan turned away and started heading for the kitchen, hoping she could run away from the conversation.

"Dearie . . . you're hiding something." Joe followed her. "If it's about me, don't you feel I should know?"

"Well, Father, you have so much to worry about and I'm certain this is just one of those silly misunderstandings that will blow over. One of the calls for Monsignor Flannagan was a woman; she didn't leave her name, but I told her Monsignor was away. And she said it was no wonder he was sick when his senior

76

assistant spends so much time away from the rectory. Well, I thought maybe she was referring to Father George; but then she said that Father Newman had been seen keeping company with a lady friend and it was a disgrace. She kept insisting on talking to Monsignor Flannagan, but when I told her it was impossible she said somebody should hear about this matter. You don't think she may have — "

"Don't jump to conclusions, Dearie. This kind of nonsense doesn't deserve this much concern. The bishop probably just wants to discuss who he will be sending to look after St. Monica's while Monsignor Flannagan's away. Just forget about this whole thing." *(I wish I could.)*

Joe wished he had not committed himself last week to have lunch and play tennis today, but he had not foreseen so many unexpected events cropping up on his day off. When he returned Father Wilson's call, the housekeeper informed him that Father Wilson had left a message for Joe to meet him and a few other former classmates at Tony's for lunch.

"Sorry I'm late. You guys haven't eaten yet, have you?" Joe asked as he pulled up a chair.

"No, we've only been here fifteen minutes and Mario hasn't taken our order yet. Want a drink?" one of them said, motioning to the waiter at the same time. Mario took the orders while Joe explained and made his apologies.

"We only have three for tennis this afternoon since Ed's away on retreat," Father Wilson said.

"You only have two, Mike. I can't play this afternoon. With Monsignor in the hospital and all the calls coming in about one thing or another, I better stick around the rectory. It's been one of those days . . . one heck of a night too." Joe began to recount his middle-of-the-night phone call, when he caught the eye of one of his parishioners who was walking toward him. It was Mrs. Ferris. *(What's she doing here? Oh, no, she's coming this way!)*

Mrs. Ferris was a thin woman with gray hair and thick framed glasses. Her thin lips pursed as she addressed the two other priests at the table: "Good afternoon, Fathers. It's so nice to see all of you enjoying your leisure." She forced a smile and motioned to Joe. "Will you excuse Father Newman for just a moment? I would like to speak to him." She had all the formality of a librarian stamping a book return. She then turned to Joe and asked him to follow her. He complied and sat at the table with her in the corner. He had all the appearance of the little boy whose book was past due. *(What does she want now? Couldn't she have waited to call me at the rectory?)*

"I don't know exactly how to say this, Father . . ." Her voice faltered momentarily.

"Say what?"

"Well . . . this isn't easy for me, but I feel this is my duty as a good Catholic. And in my conscience, I am coming straight to you with the problem, no matter how embarrassing it is for me. I do hope you understand."

"I'm trying to, if you would just tell me."

She sat back straight in her chair and folded her hands sternly on the table. "Father, I want to warn you of the gossip in the parish . . ." *(Oh, no, she's heard it too! It must be all over by now. This is just what I needed.)*

"Just this morning, Father, I heard it said that you were keeping very late hours and . . . well, that you must have some problems. You know what I mean?" She leaned forward confidentially.

"Not quite, but please go on."

"This isn't easy for me. I do hope you understand that I don't believe it for a minute; but I heard that just last Sunday night you were seen in a very bad district of the town picking up a girl, and later you were seen parked in the car with her. Mind you, I don't believe it but I did think you should know what's being said."

Joe was about to explain the real situation, but she interrupted him. "And then there was last night . . ." *(This is a new one . . . now what?)*

"What about last night?" he cut in somewhat impatiently.

"Forgive me . . . I shouldn't have said 'last night'; it was early this morning. Father, you were seen in a very inebriated state." Mrs. Ferris' voice changed from a very apologetic narrative to almost an accusing one. "It was said that you have been drinking far too much and that you were sick right out in the open by your car in a parking lot. Also, that you were out all night and you —"

Joe didn't let her finish. "Thank you, Mrs. Ferris. I don't need to hear anymore."

"But Father, I'm only doing my duty as a Christian. As I said before, I don't believe it for a moment. You know how people talk and —"

Joe excused himself and walked away; he knew he was about to react, and he was too tired and much too angry at this moment to react like a priest.

"I don't believe it, but I wanted you to know. I was only doing my duty. And you know how people talk," she called after him.

Joe downed his drink and reached in his pocket for enough money to cover his order. "I'm afraid something has come up. I have to get back to the rectory. I'll see you guys later. Sorry about this . . ."

"What's up?" Mike asked as Joe walked away.

"It's one of those days, Mike. I'll give you a call tomorrow and explain. See you guys later."

"You're back from lunch already, Father?" Mrs. Quinlan asked as Joe walked into the kitchen.

Joe nodded. "I'm going to lie down for a while, Dearie. If there are any calls, check them with George first, will you? And don't disturb me unless it's an emergency, okay?"

"Fine, Father. Do you want me to wake you at any special time? You're still having dinner at your mother's tonight, aren't you?"

"That's right . . . almost forgot. Call me at four."

"Is there anything else I can do?" Dearie asked, showing real concern. "I can tell you're upset." Then suddenly she remembered. "Oh, Father, Sister Jeanine called a little while ago. She wants you to come over to the school. She's having some problems."

"She's not the only one with problems. They can wait!" Joe said abruptly. He went to his room and lay across the bed. (I

79

don't remember seeing anyone from the parish at the hospital this morning. And what would they be doing there at four in the morning to begin with? Unless of course they work there. But still how could they say I was in an inebriated state — just because I got sick in the parking lot? Somebody must be out to really nail me. God, this must be getting to me . . . now I sound paranoid! How do you fight something like this!)

Joe's mother was a young-looking sixty even though she was already gray. She was small with the same attractive features of her son. "You're troubled, son," she said as she walked into the living room where Joe was sprawled out in a reclining chair in front of the T.V. He had removed his jacket, collar and shoes. He was so engrossed in the news he hadn't even heard her enter the room.

"Can you take time out from the world affairs, and talk to your mother?" She said as she turned the volume lower, then pulled up a chair by her son. "I asked if you were troubled."

"Just a lot on my mind." Joe replied, turning his attention away from the T.V. and facing his mother.

"Want to get it off your chest?" Mrs. Newman never received an answer. Instead Joe jumped from the recliner and raced toward the T.V. to turn the volume up. "What on earth . . ." Mrs. Newman was stunned.

"Shhh, Mom. Look!" Joe said excitedly.

On the screen there was a film spot showing the demonstration that had taken place in front of the chancery that very afternoon. Leading the demonstration was a group of young priests. "Oh my God! There's George!" Joe backed into his chair, never taking his eyes from the screen. "God, no, they're going to interview him!" Joe moved in closer as he watched the reporter hold the microphone to George. George gave a heated opinion about how he thought it was too bad that the Church had not spoken up about the war and that perhaps this kind of demonstration would move them to take action. The reporter then asked him if he felt the Church's apathy was attributed to a few of the hierarchy or whether it was the Church in general.

"Keep your mouth shut, George!" Joe screamed at the

screen. George went on to say that many in the Church shared his views and the views of other clergymen who felt the war should come to an end, but they were afraid to speak up for fear of some of the higher-ups. His own bishop had forbade them to meddle in political affairs.

Joe railed, "That's enough, George! Now shut up!" Mrs. Newman simply stared at her son. George continued to reveal that he personally didn't care what some of his superiors said . . . including the bishop. His conscience told him to do everything in his power to stop innocent people from being killed every day and if demonstrating before the chancery office would help to persuade the Church to come out and take a stand, then he would continue to do so regardless of the consequences. The reporter thanked George, turned to the camera and continued the report while George could be seen lifting his sign that read: "Speak Up Against the War!"

Joe slumped in his chair. "We haven't heard the end of this," he said as he got up and headed for the phone to call the rectory. Mrs. Quinlan informed him that George hadn't returned since he left that morning, but that she had just watched the news with Father Benetti. "If he comes in, tell him to wait for me. I'll be home right after dinner."

"And here I am holding tickets to the best seats for tonight's hockey game," Mr. Newman proclaimed as he held up the tickets.

Joe looked up with a start. "I didn't hear you come in, Dad. I'm sorry. I wish I could take advantage of them, but I have a feeling that phone will be coming off the hook tonight at St. Monica's . . . I better be there." Joe gave his father a masculine hug as if he were trying to ease his disappointment.

"Well, at least you can stay long enough to enjoy your dinner, Joe. I made chicken and dumplings, your favorite," Mrs. Newman said as she led the two men to the kitchen.

After Joe's father said grace, Mrs. Newman passed Joe the platter of chicken, saying, "Joe, could you do me a favor? You remember Mrs. Sullivan's Jennie?" Joe nodded. *(How can I ever forget her?)*

"Well," his mother continued, "the poor thing is having such

81

a rough time of it since her husband left her and the kids. Honestly, I don't know how any man could just pick up and leave such a beautiful wife and three great children." *(She was beautiful all right.)*

Mrs. Newman paused for a sip of water, then proceeded: "Her mother was telling me just this afternoon how depressed Jennie has been. It's been six months now since he left and it's so hard on her — having to work every day, then come home to keep up with the apartment and the children. I feel so sorry for her. And to think she can never marry again and she's only thirty years old. That was a valid marriage in the eyes of the Church. Remember her wedding? Didn't she make a beautiful bride?" Joe nodded but kept right on eating; he was trying to appear indifferent.

"I was thinking," she went on as she buttered a slice of bread, "maybe you could go over and talk to her. Mrs. Sullivan said she has been talking with a priest about the matter; but I think she would welcome an old friend. You two always got on well together."

"I think Joe was sweet on her, weren't you, Joe?" his father teased.

"Don't talk silly . . . they were just good friends," Mrs. Newman defended.

"I'm not being silly. Tell us the truth: you were sweet on Jennie for a while, weren't you Joe?"

"Pass the dumplings, Dad," Joe grinned as he looked at his father.

"Do you think you could just pop in for a minute?" Mrs. Newman persisted. "When a person has had the kind of luck that Jennie has, it's always a consolation to know you still have old friends who care."

"I'll see, Mom, but I've been running a tight schedule lately and with Monsignor Flannagan in the hospital, it's going to get tighter. Besides, if she's already talking to a priest, I don't want to interfere with his counsel." *(That's a flimsy excuse . . . I hope she buys it and drops the whole thing.)*

Throughout the short drive home, Joe's thoughts volleyed

from George and his demonstration to Jennie and her dilemma. It was more pleasant to just recall the times he and Jennie shared than to dwell on her present problem, but the mere mention of her name had unlocked a thousand pleasant memories, ones that Joe had tucked away for a long time. He wondered if she was still as beautiful as she was eleven years ago. *(Maybe a bad marriage and three kids have taken their toll on her? Wonder if she still laughs the same and bites her thumbnail when she's listening closely . . . or if her hair is still fixed the same, or if she still has a passion for french fries and cherry cokes . . . I wonder what she's like now?)*

The softness of Joe's fantasies were brought to an abrupt halt as he pulled into the rectory drive and peered out at the cold stone structure of St. Monica's that seemed to be looking down on him almost chastisingly, bringing him back to reality.

"Father Rahner isn't back yet and the phone's been going constantly," Dearie exclaimed as she met Joe at the door. Joe was expecting this.

"I'll handle the rest of the calls, Dearie. I'll take the phone in the office, but as soon as George gets back, ask him to see me, will you?"

"Father Benetti went to his room. He said he didn't want to have anything to do with this whole thing with Father George. There's been a lot of calls for Father George too. I just acted like nothing happened and told them to leave their number and he would call them."

"Fine. You did the right thing," Joe said as he started down the hall.

By ten the phone stopped ringing, but Joe was still waiting for George. Mrs. Quinlan and Father Benetti had both retired for the night. Joe called his brother, Tim, to see how Kate was doing. Tim assured him that everything was getting back to order in the Newman household, but that he still hadn't told his wife about his plans for a vasectomy. Joe tried to persuade him to reconsider and Tim agreed that he would, but as Joe hung up the phone, he wasn't too certain that his brother was just trying to pacify him.

Joe checked the television schedule for a good movie. He

83

switched the channel to a science-fiction story, glanced at his watch, then waited.

Finally at about 12:30 George's car pulled into the drive. Joe rose to meet him. He sat back down quickly; he didn't want to appear overanxious. He lit a cigarette and tried to affect a non-chalant attitude as George entered.

"Did you see it?" George asked as he took a chair beside Joe.

"I saw it. You're very photogenic."

"That's not all you have to say though, is it?"

"Looks like you kind of said it all. There's been quite a reaction, judging from the calls that came to the rectory tonight."

"Pro or con?"

"Both. But the opinions of the callers aren't that important. The chancery office's opinions are, and judging how you really let go today, I'd say theirs aren't going to be too favorable."

"I know. I got carried away a little. But I'm not sorry I said what I did. Somebody has to. What I said was the truth. And I'll take the responsibility for it." George's voice held conviction.

"Then you are prepared for a reaction from them?"

"Of course. I know what I'm doing. No reason for you to be uptight though. I'm the one who's going to be called on the carpet — not you."

"I just wanted to warn you," Joe explained. This was a new role for Joe, but he felt he must share some of the responsibility for his associate since he really wondered if George was totally aware of his imprudence.

"Don't worry, Joe. But thanks for being concerned." George started for his room, then turned back. "Hey, you didn't wait up for me, did you?"

Joe realized he was appearing to be somewhat of a "mother hen" and he felt a little embarrassed. "Oh, no, I got interested in a movie . . . couldn't turn it off." Joe directed his attention back to the screen, but he hadn't the slightest idea what was happening in the plot.

Joe had another cigarette before he turned in for the night. *(I feel badly about putting Mom off that way regarding Jennie.)* His mind ran back to his last summer at home before he returned to the seminary for ordination. That summer would ·

84

always be special to him. He was certain God planned it that way. Up until then, there was never a real doubt that he wanted only the priesthood. God must have sent Jennie that summer to make him realize that nothing anyone really wants can be his without sacrifice. That summer he wanted Jennie too . . . but couldn't have both. Nevertheless, he made his choice. How he enjoyed being with her; she seemed to understand his every mood, and he, hers. She was warm and sensitive one minute, giggly and fickle the next. *(And those eyes . . . you could get lost in them. Her husband must have been a fool to leave her . . . what more would any man want in a woman? Maybe Mom was right. Maybe I should pay her a visit . . . just a call to see how she's getting along wouldn't hurt. And maybe I could help her through her problems. But would I be going to "really" help her? . . . or just to see her again?)* Joe felt a warm glow as he recalled her every feature. He enjoyed his thoughts until another struck him . . . *(I better "stay out of the bakery!")* Joe tossed in his bed, and all his thoughts seemed to center on Tom Baxter. *(What's it all about Lord? . . . Death. We all must die. How many more Tom Baxters, soldiers, war victims . . . and people like Flannagan. All must die . . . but not just them. All of us will die . . . when, we don't know. Maybe that's why we become priests, to make sense of death by preaching eternal life!)*

CHAPTER 5

THINGS OLD AND NEW

(Thursday a.m.)

"Don't forget to stop for a few moments after Mass to see Sister Jeanine, Father Newman. I think she's a little upset because you didn't return her call yesterday afternoon. She says it's very important," Mrs. Frye, the school secretary, reminded Joe as he was entering the church for the eight o'clock Mass.

"Tell her I'll be there first thing." (*I'm in no mood to listen to her petty problems about the kids' behavior. I wish I had more time to talk with George again before he left for the university . . . he'll probably be gone by the time I finish Mass. I don't suppose there's much I can say to him anyway. I wonder what Flannagan's reaction is going to be . . . it's a cinch he'll find out about it. I don't know why I'm worried . . . it's as George said last night: he did it, not me, and he's ready to accept the responsibility. I guess that it's just that I don't think George is too sure of himself in other things regarding the priesthood . . . but there I go judging again.*)

After Mass Joe entered the anteroom of the principal's office where Mrs. Frye was busy typing. "Sister Jeanine is waiting for you," she said with a grin as he passed her desk.

"Thank you, Mrs. Frye." He opened the door to the principal's room; there pulling the blinds at the window, with her back to him, was a red-haired woman in a short blue dress. "Sorry," Joe said and shut the door without entering. He turned to the secretary. "I thought you said Sister Jeanine was waiting

for me," he said in a muffled but embarrassed tone of voice.
"I did!" she giggled.

The principal's door opened. "Come in, Father." It was Sister Jeanine, but she wasn't in her habit.

Joe followed her into the office a little dumbfounded. He realized he had forgotten to shut the door behind him; when he turned around, he caught sight of Mrs. Frye trying to stifle her laughter with a handkerchief held tightly to her mouth. He felt silly as he took the chair across from the principal's desk. Sister Jeanine gave him no time to explain his reaction. She took her chair and folded her hands, very businesslike, on her desk pad. "Father, I have a problem," she stated firmly.

Joe squelched his desire to say, "You certainly do!" Instead he cleared his throat and answered, "Yes, Sister, and I'm very sorry I didn't return your call yesterday. It slipped my mind." Joe found it difficult to concentrate on the conversation. He had never imagined her as having "red" hair.

"That's not important, now. You're here and I'm glad. There are several things I want to discuss with you." *(I bet I know what one of them is.)* "I'm glad I can tell you directly instead of on the phone." Her voice remained extremely professional.

"Well, I'm here. What's your problem, Sister?" *(As if I didn't know.)* Joe was trying hard to match her professional manner, but the picture before his eyes was just too amusing. Sister Jeanine had "red" hair and it was curled too!

"First off . . . there's the discipline in the school, or should I say the 'lack of it' that has me upset." She stiffened up and paused a moment, then continued, "Frankly, Father, I feel you're largely to blame."

"Me? Why me?"

"Father Newman, I wish I didn't have to remind you that we have a schedule to keep in this school. You cancel your classes without a minute's notice, then the teachers have to change their plans without any warning. This can cause a tremendous amount of interference with the overall curriculum."

"I understand, Sister, but unfortunately my duties take me other places besides this school and sometimes, I have no warning of a change in my plans either."

"I'm aware of that, Father. However, all I'm asking is that you cooperate with us as best you can. Actually that isn't the main problem. Even when you are in the school, you tend to disrupt the schedule by running overtime in the different classes; the schedule is still not kept. Father, we cannot run a well-disciplined school like that. I believe you allow the children far too much freedom. You permit them to take advantage of you by allowing them almost playground freedom in the classroom even while you are teaching them. The teachers find it almost impossible to restore order after you've left."

"Forgive me, Sister ... but I would hardly call letting the children discuss and ask questions openly, 'playground freedom,'" Joe said in his own defense. *(I bet if she had the chance, she would join Women's Lib. I can picture her as chairman of the whole organization ... red hair and all.)*

"Father, you can't deny that when you enter a classroom, some of the children leave their desks and run to you and tug, and jump around, and laugh, and —"

"No, I can't deny that, but I do restore order, and get down to the business of teaching religion, do I not?"

"Yes, Father," Sister Jeanine conceded. "No one is questioning your ability as a teacher. It's just that the children get so excited and the teachers find it hard to control them after you leave."

"I can only be responsible for what happens while I'm there, Sister," Joe smiled. *(Man, am I glad there are no "lady bishops!")*

"I don't want to sound like a dictator, but we do have rules and rules must be kept!" Her voice had become very stern, and her face rigid. *(When is she going to get around to the habit business? I'll show her ... I'm not going to give her the satisfaction by even bringing it up.)*

Sister Jeanine's voice softened to a more feminine tone. "How is the monsignor?" she asked, suddenly changing the subject.

"He's feeling a little sore this morning, I imagine, with just having the surgery yesterday. I'll tell him you asked about him."

"Please do. Will you be talking with him today?" *(Here it comes. She wants me to do her dirty work for her and tell the boss about the new clothes . . . no wonder she's becoming a little more mellow.)*

"I'll probably talk to him some time today. Do you have any messages?"

"Well, you might mention that we've changed our dress. I know I made an agreement with him about the habits, but at the time I didn't realize that we would feel pressure from the rest of our community. You see, we really should try to keep unity in the order . . . and we Sisters here at St. Monica's were the last ones to change over. Actually, since I knew we had to make the change sooner or later, I felt it best to do it while he was away . . . to kind of get over the parish reaction, I mean. You understand, don't you Father?"

Joe smiled. *(Now she's on the defensive.)* "So you want me to tell Monsignor Flannagan for you?" She smiled sweetly and nodded affirmatively. "And the rest of the parish . . . what shall I tell them when they discover your change, especially when they ask why you Sisters feel lay clothes are better than habits?"

Sister Jeanine rose and stood directly in front of him. "Just tell them that we want to be thought of as women — women who want to relate!" *(There's that "Women's Lib" voice again.)*

"I'll quote you, Sister, and I'll try to help the school schedule and discipline run more smoothly." Joe rose to leave. "And in the meantime, I want to wish you luck . . . relating!"

Joe rushed back to the rectory for a quick breakfast before he took the morning religion classes. George's car was still in the drive. *(Good. George must have decided not to take his classes today . . . that was using good judgment. Or maybe this is just his day off? At any rate, I'm glad . . . maybe he can sit by the phone for a change.)*

Joe could hear Father Benetti's shrill voice babbling with amazing speed in Italian when he walked through the rectory door. There stood the old priest in the middle of the kitchen waving his arms frantically as he continued to shout. Every sentence would start off in English, but end in Italian. Mrs. Quinlan was trying to calm him by offering him a cup of tea. They made a comic scene: Father Benetti, in his cassock and black hat which he had forgotten to remove, and Mrs. Quinlan trying to balance the hot cup of tea, long enough to reach its destination, by dodging Father Benetti's swinging arms. When Joe shut the door, they both stopped right where they were to see who had entered; when they realized it was just Joe, they both continued their conversation. "What's happening?" Joe asked, amused.

Father Benetti raised his hands to his ears and rocked his head from side to side. Finally, he sat down at the table and began sipping his drink. He was still wearing his hat, only now it was tilted to the side of his head.

"Father Benetti forgot his breviary this morning; he left it in the sacristy so he decided to go over and get it just a few minutes ago. When he went to the church, he ran into two of our Sisters taking the children in for choir practice. Father is upset about the nuns." Dearie smiled and winked at Joe over Father Benetti's shoulder.

Hearing the explanation, the old priest started in once again . . . English first, then Italian.

"You're going to have to stay with the English, Father," Joe quipped as he took a chair at the table.

"Did you see them? What are they doing? We already have a shortage of nuns and they want to look like we have less than we do. Did you see them?"

"Yes, just a minute ago — "

"Well, what do *you* think?"

"I must say I was surprised, but I suppose they know what they're doing."

"You mean you agree with what they're doing, giving up their religious habits?" Father Benetti was becoming more upset.

"Not exactly, Father. I may be progressive as far as theology is concerned, but I'm still conservative enough to feel that nuns should look like nuns." Joe sipped his coffee.

"I'm so upset . . . I can't even pray. What's St. Monica's coming to? We have a 'T.V. star' as an assistant and a bunch of women running around like salesladies calling themselves nuns. Why do they do it? Can you answer that? *Mamma Mia perche!*" He threw his arms in the air.

"To quote Sister Jeanine: they 'want to be thought of as

women, women who want to relate!' " Joe was certain this statement would not calm the old priest and he was sorry he had even said it.

" 'Relate'! Relate to whom? The hippies?" Father Benetti was shouting again. "Or maybe they can relate to the priests who think that carrying signs up and down the street is more important than tending to the needs of their parishioners. What is happening to St. Monica's? What is happening to the Church? The world? Everybody wants to relate. Now the nuns want to relate. Well, they don't relate to me and they won't relate to the monsignor . . . and they won't relate to ninety percent of the people in this parish!" He paused long enough to catch his breath. "I just hope they relate to God . . . that's Whom they're supposed to be working for . . . or has that changed too?" Father Benetti was being sarcastic, but sarcasm from him proved comical, especially since his hat was still tilted on his head.

George entered the kitchen and poured himself a cup of coffee. "What are you doing home?" Joe asked.

"I didn't have the first two classes this morning, so I decided to stay home and catch up on some reading; but when I heard all this 'relating' going on in here, I thought I might sit in to see if I could find something to relate to," he teased.

"Ah . . . now we have an authority. *A hippie priest!*" Father Benetti said as he nudged Joe and motioned towards George. "I suppose you agree with the Sisters giving up their religious habits? "What *do* you think of them?"

"Groovy!"

"What did he say?" Father Benetti practically bellowed at Joe. "What is this 'groovy' supposed to mean?"

Joe was about to answer when George interrupted. "It means that I'm glad to see 'they're doing their own thing!' "

" 'Doing their own thing'?" Father Benetti's voice rose several more decibels. "Tell me, is this the new language of the Church? You must inform me, Father; I've been a priest for fifty years, but I have never before heard about the nuns 'doing their own thing! Maybe this is all a part of the new Church . . . priests demonstrating like workers on strike . . . nuns dressing like salesladies . . . 'doing their own thing' . . . Bah!"

"At least we're doing something. Anything that will make people aware of the world around them and their responsibility as a part of it is worthwhile doing. We must make people aware of what's happening now!" George argued.

Father Benetti sat back in his chair with a look of defeat, his hat still tilted on his head. He presented the image of a Little Leaguer who had just struck out his last time at bat. He picked up his drink and started for his room. "It used to be such a nice Church," he said despondently.

"I guess I shook the old boy up," George shrugged. "I was just telling it like it is."

Joe didn't know if he was moved by sympathy for the old man or if it was a feeling that George owed the old priest more respect; but he found himself, nevertheless, speaking up in Father Benetti's behalf.

"You may have shaken him, but you will never shake his faith . . . which is more than I can say for many of you guys who go around waving a flag and screaming their cause to anyone they can find that will listen. And I'll tell you another thing. While a lot of you are protesting the war by walking the streets carrying your signs, then going home to your comfortable rooms, you will never know, with the help of God, what it means to go from foxhole to foxhole giving the last rites, or leading a bunch of half-starved, war-stricken kids into bomb shelters, or offering the Mass on the rubble left by bombs, or spend weeks in an army hospital recovering from a piece of metal lodged in your guts. But that old man has lived through all of that. You think he doesn't know what's going on around him? You think he doesn't know the horrors of war? He could tell you of atrocities, that he's not just read about, but lived through. I've got news for you, George. It's going to take a hell of a lot more than you to make that old man shake!" Joe stormed out of the kitchen.

Instead of going to his first religion class, Joe went directly to the teachers' lounge to have a cigarette, but mostly to cool off. He was glad to see the room unoccupied as he took a chair and began to page through a folder left on the table. *(I'm in no mood to teach those kids anything right now. Why do I always sound off like that? Much of what George was saying was true, yet I acted like a nut over the whole thing when it really wasn't any of my business anyway. It was between George and Benetti. God, I've got to calm down. I'm letting everything that's happened in the past few days cloud my judgment about everything.)* Joe folded his hands under his chin and closed his eyes as if he were trying to pray. *(Put me in the right frame of mind to teach those kids, Lord. Don't let my doubts and worries interfere with my obligation to them.)*

As Joe was shutting the door of the lounge, a little first-grader was just leaving the boys' lavatory. "Hi, Father Joe!" He ran towards Joe with his arms outstretched. When he smiled, he displayed the void of a front tooth. Joe picked the youngster up and swung him around, then placed him back to a standing position as he grabbed his shoulders. "What happened to your tooth? Got in a fight, I'll bet."

"No, just fell out."

"If you promise not to tell anyone, I'll tell you a secret. The tooth fairy called me last night and told me that if I saw Larry Kramer today, I should give him this to buy an ice cream after school." Joe held out a quarter in the palm of his hand.

The boy smiled widely. "I don't believe in that stuff anymore, Father."

"Then I guess you don't want the ice cream?"

"Sure, I want the ice cream . . . but you're just putting me on about the tooth fairy."

"I guess I can't fool you, huh, Larry? Well, take the ice cream money anyway." Someone clearing his throat very exaggeratingly diverted Joe's attention from the little boy. He turned to find Sister Jeanine standing at the end of the hall.

"Run along to your room now, Larry," Joe said. "I'll see you later." Joe ducked into the eighth-grade classroom. Sister Gregory rose from her desk and motioned to the class to rise also as he entered. "Good morning, Father," they all cried in unison. Sister Gregory was wearing a beige knit dress and brown heels. *(My God . . . she has blond hair! It's too blond to be real . . . maybe not, she has a fair complexion. I wonder if she dyed it for the occasion??? No . . . that's stupid, nuns don't dye their hair . . . at least they never used to . . . .)*

"Good morning, kids. Good morning, Sister Gregory," he said as he took his place behind the desk.

"It's Sister Mary Jane now, Father," the young nun said softly.

"Sister Mary Jane?"

"Yes, you see we were granted permission to use our baptismal names if we wished, so I went back to mine." *(Figures, she looks more like a "Mary Jane" than a "Gregory.")*

"New dress, new name, huh, Sister?" Joe smiled. *(Wonder if it's new hair too.)* He reached for the question box on the desk as he watched Sister Gregory *(... Whoops! Sister Mary Jane ...)* walk to the back of the room. *(New walk too!)*

Joe found the question box in the upper grades to be the best tool for teaching. He could create discussion and oftentimes he found that the kids had more serious questions than he really gave them credit for. He knew also that many times the question box was used simply to find out more about Father Joe and his opinions than about religion. He reached for the first question, then read it aloud: "Why don't Catholics read the Bible as much as Protestants?"

Joe answered, "Catholics should read the Bible as much as Protestants, but we depend on the Church to interpret for us instead of interpreting it for ourselves. The Catholic Church is a teaching Church. Also, let me remind you that in every Mass there is a reading from the Bible and many of the phrases we use in the Proper of the Mass are taken from Scripture. For instance...." Joe went on to cite different examples of quotations, then tell the stories from which they were taken from the Scriptures.

Next question: "If a priest leaves the priesthood and gets married, can he still go to the sacraments?"

Joe explained that if a priest went through the right channels, he could become dispensed from his vows, but this took much time and many things had to be considered. However, if he were officially laicized, he would be free to attend the sacraments. The children seemed to be quite surprised at this one, and it triggered a long and animated discussion.

"We only have time for one more question," Joe said, reaching in the box. He read the question silently. *(Here's another one of those.)* The question was: "What do *you* think of french kissing?" Joe knew that their classes in sex education were quite elaborate and that they had covered this thoroughly. He felt certain that this question had been put in there either because they "liked to talk about it" or perhaps to study his reaction. Joe knew how to handle this one. He read the question aloud, "What do you think of french kissing?" Joe folded the paper carefully and answered, "I never think of it!" then made his way to the door to the howls and giggles of the class.

"Thank you, Father, that was a very interesting session," Sister Mary Jane said as she opened the door for him to leave. Joe looked at her closely, smiled and left the room. *(Well, if she ever decides to leave the convent she can always get a job doing commercials for toothpaste. She seems to have all the requirements . . . and a nice smile.)*

"Father Newman, Mrs. Quinlan just called the school office and asked that you return to the rectory right away. You had a very important call and it couldn't wait," Mrs. Frye said as she met him in the hall, a little breathless.

"Thanks. Better tell Sister Jeanine that I may be tied up again."

"Here's the number you should call. It was Mrs. Davis. She was crying and I could hardly make heads or tails from what she was saying. But she did say it was an emergency." Mrs. Quinlan handed him the note pad and pointed out the number as Joe started dialing the telephone.

"She said it was an emergency?"

"Yes, Father . . . terribly upset she was too." *(Not another "emergency.")* Joe could picture the scene that awaited him as he thought of the last time he heard that expression used on the phone. Again the image of Tom's burnt flesh forced its way into his mind like a flash of lightning.

The line was busy. Joe sat down impatiently and began to tap his fingers on the kitchen table where Father Benetti had left his breviary opened that morning. Joe began to read and meditate at the same time about how difficult it used to be when

95

the breviary had to be read in Latin . . . but it still wasn't any easier in English. The office never seemed to fit his moods — for when he was feeling depressed, the writer was gushing with joy; but when he was elated the readings seemed weary and vengeful. He tried the number again . . . still busy. *(What is she doing on the phone if she's waiting for me to call?)* He continued to read: Have mercy on me, O God, in the greatness of your compassion wipe out my offense. Thoroughly wash me from my guilt and of my sin cleanse me. For I acknowledge my offense and my sin is before me always. *(I guess that was meaningful to David. After all, he had committed adultery and murder, but it's hard for me to get his feeling of remorse over impatience and an occasional loss of temper.)*

Joe tried the number again; this time it was ringing. "Hello, Mrs. Davis, it's Father Newman." Before Joe could say anything else, he heard her sobs coming across the line, then finally, "It's Pam, Father. She's gone."

"Mrs. Davis . . . try to calm down and explain your problem to me as clearly as you can."

"Pam's been gone since Tuesday night. I thought everything was going well. We took your advice and went to see that priest you mentioned. Pam wasn't happy when he advised her to stay away from the boy because he wasn't a good influence; but she said she would think about it and I had hoped that she would settle down some. But I guess she's not going to do what we asked of her after all . . ."

"Do you have any idea where she may be?"

"I found out just now from a girlfriend of Pam's that she was seen in the worst part of town with a bunch of hippies and . . ." More sobs.

For the next five minutes Joe listened to an incoherent account between sobbing and sniffling, a great feat of patience for a man who constantly acknowledged his lack of it. *(So she was seen in the worst part of town with some hippies. Not surprising since most hippie types feel the same way as Pam does about life . . . birds of a feather . . .)* Joe doodled a bird on the note pad as he listened.

Mrs. Davis blew her nose loudly and Joe held the phone

away from his ear a second. She continued. "I don't know whether to call the police or not . . . the scandal, you know."

"If she's been gone since Tuesday night, why have you waited so long to do something?"

"I just found out last night . . . and my husband and I took the first plane home to —"

"Wait a minute," Joe interrupted impatiently. "You mean you were out of town?"

"Yes . . . Father. I just had to get away from all of this and since Walter was going away for a convention to Miami, I thought I would take the opportunity to go with him. I thought maybe a few days in the sun with friends might help me to —"

"Then you left Pam alone?" Joe's face turned scarlet as he tried to control his temper.

"The housekeeper stayed on and when I called home Tuesday night, she said Pam left with a suitcase and there was nothing she could do to stop her. I'm so upset. Walter said he's going to call the police — and, Father, I just don't know what to do. Trying to keep this pregnancy a secret will be difficult enough as it is and now he wants to call — "

"Then what do you want me to do?" Joe broke in as his exasperation mounted.

There was no answer for a minute. He waited for Mrs. Davis to finish blowing her nose again. "I wonder if you could find her and speak to her before the police do. I think I know where she is, but I haven't told anyone. Lord knows we have enough scandal on our hands. If you could — "

Joe didn't wait for her to finish. "Mrs. Davis, don't you think we could save some time if you gave me the address of where you think she may be?" Joe drew a circle around the bird on the doodling pad as Mrs. Davis rattled on and on about how she couldn't call there since the party didn't have a phone and how embarrassed she's been over the whole mess. By the time she finally gave him the address, of which she wasn't too certain, and the name of the young man of which she was equally uncertain, Joe had drawn an elaborate bird cage and a cat waiting to pounce.

CHAPTER 6

JUDGE NOT

(Thursday p.m.)

Joe didn't have too much to go on as he drove to the house where Mrs. Davis "thought" Pam may be. She was sure that Jack lived on this street, but she didn't know the boy's last name for certain since she only heard Pam use it a couple of times as far as she could remember. She only knew that he lived on Ninth Street because one of Pam's girl friends had told her. She had also said that she wasn't certain where Jack lived on that block, but she did know of an apartment house on Ninth Street — 2914, to be precise — where the kids who wanted to really swing could get *anything* . . . uppers, downers, the works. It would appear they could do anything they wanted. Joe wasn't too easy about how far to take the last statement, especially since he was getting the report secondhand from Mrs. Davis. *(This must be it. Man, is this place run down. I hope my car will be okay . . . I better make sure I leave it locked up.)* The sidewalks were littered with trash and a group of longhairs and their female counterparts stood on the corner. *(Can hardly tell which is which. They're all dressed the same . . . dirty, unwashed and beaded.)*

Joe parked the car by the entrance and locked it. He felt self-conscious as he walked up the steps wearing sneakers, a yellow turtleneck, and a light-blue jacket. *(It wouldn't be good to be seen entering these doors wearing a Roman collar. It wouldn't be good to be seen entering these doors, period. If Mrs. Ferris could see me now!)*

The smell of stale liquor and filth grabbed him as he entered the foyer. Joe scanned the shabby mail slots hoping to find a name he could apply to Jack. He had his choice of three: J. Kraischely, John Aubuschon, or J. Montag. *(I guess I'll have to try all three. You would think Davis would have found out for sure the name of his expected grandchild. Maybe Pam just didn't want to give them that information. I'll bluff my way and ask for Pam. J. Kraischely lives on the first floor, let's start from there.)* He knocked on the door and waited. A woman he judged to be in her late twenties, clad in a loud Jersey mini, answered. Joe felt he had made the wrong choice even before he asked, "Is Pam here?"

"She ain't staying here, handsome. She's up there and she's booked. Anything I can do for you? Got more experience." She slid closer to Joe and rested her wrists on his shoulders.

Joe felt the color come to his cheeks as he pulled her wrists away. He walked away without saying a word and started up the dingy staircase.

"You'll find what you're looking for on the third floor, room 6, sweetie," she called after him.

At the top of the staircase sat a little girl; she was pathetically thin and uncared for. "Hi, look what I did!" she said, smiling, and held up a coloring book.

"That's very nice. Did you do that all by yourself?" Joe asked, stooping over the child.

"Uh-huh," she answered proudly.

The door behind her swung open and a woman reached out and grabbed the child's arm, dragging her through the doorway. "What the hell you doin' hangin' around my kid?" She yelled at him suspiciously. "Beat it!" She slammed the door.

Joe felt sick over the woman's insinuation as he hurried up the steps to the third floor. Room 6 had no name on the door. He could hear music coming from within as he knocked. A young man in his thirties answered. He was wearing tight pink pants and a puffed sleeve shirt that was open to the waist; he had on brown eyeshadow and held a long cigarette holder. "Well, well, look what Santa's brought . . . you big hunk of cheesecake . . . do come in." He held his left hand on his hip as he drew in on the cigarette and blew a puff of smoke into Joe's face, winking at the same time. Before Joe was able to recover from the shock, the doorway was crowded with equally feminine and even more ostentatious young men. *(So that's what the gal on the first floor meant when she told me I could find what I was looking for up here. She thinks I'm queer simply because I rejected her advances.)* Joe didn't know how to extricate himself gracefully so he swallowed hard and said, "Sorry, wrong room," and made off accompanied by the whistles and wolf calls of the laughing young men.

Joe went back to the second floor and knocked on the door where one John Aubuschon supposedly resided. A young girl, about seventeen, answered. "Is Pam here?" Joe asked.

"Who are you?"

"A friend. Is she here?"

"I don't know if she wants to see you," the girl answered nervously.

"Look, if she's here, will you tell her that Father Newman is here and I just want to talk to her . . . please?"

"Wait a minute." The girl shut the door. Within minutes she returned. "Come on in . . . she's in the other room." The girl pointed to a doorway to what appeared to be the bedroom. Joe looked around the front room where there was just the scarcest amount of furniture. An old maroon stuffed chair was in one corner. There were several mats on the floor and a card table and three chairs against one of the walls. Posters were hanging from every wall. How could she want to live in this, Joe thought as he stepped over empty soda cans and ashtrays. "You really a priest?" the girl asked. Joe nodded and went through the doorway towards which she had pointed.

Pam was huddled on a couch; she was unbelievably pale and from the look of her eyes she must have been crying. Her arms were crossed tightly across her abdomen. All the toughness Joe had seen last Sunday was gone and instead there was the look of a frightened little girl. "Pam, I came to talk to you," he said as he pulled a small stool next to the cot.

"You don't really want to talk to me, Father," she began to cry. "I'm so ashamed."

"Pam, what's wrong with you? You look ill. Is it drugs?"

She shook her head "no" and began to cry even harder.

"Pam, don't you want to talk to me?" Joe's voice was gentle. "Are you this upset over the baby?"

"There is no baby, Father . . . not anymore." She wiped her eyes with a dirty towel that was lying on the cot.

Joe's mind was racing with a thousand questions. He took the dirty towel from her and handed her a clean handerchief from his pants pocket.

"Suppose you tell me about it."

"What's there to tell? I came here Tuesday night. I didn't want to stay at home anymore. There's nothing for me there, so I came to live with Jack. He told me he'd take care of me before. I didn't have any money or nothing but he said not to worry, that he would take care of everything. Then yesterday, he told me he was going to take me to see a friend, that he thought it all out and it was better for both of us to get rid of the baby."

"Did you want this too, Pam?" Joe's voice was still gentle; he couldn't help but pity the poor girl as she trembled pathetically.

"I didn't want to get rid of my baby, Father. Once I thought about having something of my very own to love. I think I kind of wanted it, but I didn't know what to do."

"Why didn't you go home?"

"They didn't want me there, Father. That priest you sent us to said I should stay away from Jack. When I talked to him alone for a few minutes he said that I wouldn't be giving my baby any kind of future, living from day to day, not knowing what was ahead of me. He said that I could give my baby a better future if I turned it over to Catholic Charities for adoption. So I figured I'd just have it, then give it away. But when we got home, my Mom and Dad started in again about how I shamed them and they told me I would have to go and stay at some home before I began to show. Then the next thing I knew they were both packing their bags to go to some convention. They told me to stay with the housekeeper and they would bring me something back 'very nice.' Well, the whole next day, while they were gone, I got to thinking about how I was just in the way there. And no matter what that priest said, Jack did tell me that he would take care of me. So I came here."

101

"Where's Jack now?" Joe asked.

"I don't know . . . he just said he'd be back later on tonight. He said I could stay here a few days till I felt better, then if I wanted I could go with him to L.A., or move in with the guy next door 'cause the rent will run out here soon." Pam clutched at her abdomen harder and began rocking back and forth. "I don't feel good, Father."

"Have you eaten anything today?"

"No, I didn't feel good enough to get anything and there wasn't anything here to eat."

Joe went to the other room and handed the girl a few dollars and asked her to go to the diner in the middle of the block and get some soup, a couple of sandwiches and a malt. Joe then reached in his pocket again for a couple more dollars, "Take this too so you'll be sure you have enough . . . better get yourself something to eat too."

Pam was now lying on her side, still holding her stomach, when Joe reentered the room. "I want you to eat something, then I'm taking you to a friend of mine, a doctor. You don't look so good. Who was this friend of Jack's?"

"It was an old guy, but I'm sure he was a doctor 'cause he asked me a whole bunch of questions, and he had all kinds of instruments and stuff. He said when it was all over that it was a good thing Jack brought me when he did 'cause I was over three months . . ." Pam began to cry again.

"Don't talk about it. Try to relax until the food comes. I'm going to run down the hall. I saw a phone there." Joe took Pam's hand and held it tightly. "Listen to me, honey. If I can make arrangements for you to stay with some Sisters, will you go with me?"

"Okay, Father," she sniffed. "I don't want to stay here anymore . . . Jack really doesn't love me."

Joe dialed the Convent of the Good Shepherd and talked with the mother superior. He explained the whole situation and she advised him that the procedure for admitting a girl to the home normally went through other channels, but if he felt the family would handle all the legal red tape and that Pam would come willingly, she would find a place for her. She also advised that the visiting physician was there for the afternoon and if he hurried, the doctor could check her and make a better evaluation of her condition.

The bag of food was resting on the stool, still untouched when Joe returned. "I'm sorry, Father. I just can't eat. I don't feel good . . . I'm so dizzy."

"Where's your clothes?"

Pam pointed to an open suitcase in the corner. Joe snapped the latch of the case after he tossed a few other garments, that were lying next to it, in the grip. "Can we go now, Pam?"

"I guess," she said as she stood slowly, weaving for a moment.

Joe removed his jacket and slipped it around her shoulders. "Better wear this. It's a little chilly. Can you walk all right?"

"I think so," she answered, taking Joe's arm and walking slowly out of the room.

The daylight made Pam's color even whiter; there were dark circles under her eyes and her lips were almost blue. Joe was only a few blocks away when Pam asked, "Father, when can I go to confession?"

"Right now, if you want."

For the next ten minutes, Pam poured her heart out, but she wasn't crying anymore; it seemed that she was all cried out. Joe gave her absolution and a penance although Joe felt she had provided her own penance as he watched her still tremble.

"Father?"

"Yes?"

"I wasn't just saying that . . . you know, when I said I was truly sorry for all my sins, I mean. I really am! I've never been so sorry in all my life."

"I know, Pam."

"Father?"

"Yes?"

"I really didn't want to kill my baby . . . I was so confused and so depressed, and I just — "

"Try not to think about it now." *(God, what am I saying? Try not to think that you just destroyed the life God put inside you? Just erase from your mind what the Church tells us and I*

103

believe is murder? How can I tell this girl at this moment the seriousness of her sin when she feels the gravity of it more than even I?) Joe looked at Pam when he pulled to the stoplight. She was a pretty girl even through anemic color. He wished he could say more to her, to comfort her. Suddenly the reading in the Divine Office that he had looked over when he was trying to reach her mother came to mind: "Have mercy on me, O God; in the greatness of your compassion wipe out my offense. Thoroughly wash me from my guilt and of my sin cleanse me. For I acknowledge my offense and my sin is before me always." *For my sin is before me always.* The reading did apply today; it applied to Pam.

Joe walked around to the passenger's side of the car to help Pam. "I'm scared, Father," she said as she stared at the large gray stone building.

"Don't be. Inside those cold walls are the warmest people God made. Come on, let me help you. If you're still feeling faint, you can lean on me."

"Hello, Father Newman . . . Pam," greeted the mother superior as she opened the door. *(Good, she remembered the name I gave her. That will put Pam at ease and make her relax a little.)*

"Pam, the doctor will see you right away, dear. We want to make sure you're all right, then I'll take you to your room and perhaps you can rest." The nun put her hand on Pam's shoulder and smiled softly. "Will you come with me, dear?"

Pam turned to Joe. Tears were beginning to well up in her eyes again, but much of the sadness had already left her face. "Thank you, Father." She put her arms around his neck and hugged him. He could feel the warm tears against his cheek. He held her closely and whispered, "Everything will be all right . . . wait and see. I'll stay here to make certain the doctor says you're okay." He released her and brushed her hair from her wet eyes. "Thank you, Father," she said again as she followed the nun down the hall.

"I asked the doctor to call me in my office as soon as he finished the examination. We can go in there and wait," the nun said as she returned. "We have quite an elaborate medical room downstairs, a dental room too. Sometime when things are a little less hectic, perhaps you would like to see them."

Two girls came running down the hall excitedly, screaming, "Mother! Mother Bernadette! Princess just had another puppy . . . that makes five! We're taking some warm milk to her." One girl stopped as she ran past them. "Good afternoon, Father," she said in a calmer voice, then ran on.

"You don't happen to know anybody," the nun laughed, "who's looking for a puppy, do you, Father?"

"Not offhand, but if I hear of someone, I'll send him here."

"Please do . . . we have eight dogs already. I doubt if we can accommodate five more."

"Eight?"

"Yes, we find that animals are very good for the girls. They not only enjoy the pets, but the animals' presence also gives them a sense of added responsibility . . . good therapy."

The mother superior's office was quite homey . . . not at all institution-like as Joe expected. Just as Joe and Sister took their chairs, the intercom buzzed.

"Yes?"

"Mother, we're taking some of the girls shopping. Do you need anything while we're out?"

"If you're going by the library, Sister, I would appreciate it if you would check to see if the book I've been waiting for has come in. I put my name on the list a few weeks ago and I still haven't heard."

"You mean the one on ghost stories?"

The mother superior blushed as she caught Joe smiling. "Yes, Sister, that's the one . . . and thanks." She switched off the intercom. "I have a weakness for suspense, Father. I find it relaxing."

There was a gentle knock on the door. "Excuse me, Mother, there's a gentleman at the door with three bushel baskets of apples. Did we order them?" a woman in a blue suit asked in a very low voice.

"Sister Rose ordered them for her cottage. She and her girls are planning to make apple jelly. Send him over to her cottage . . . oh, wait! Perhaps he'd best leave them at the door where the girls can pick them up later. Princess belongs to that group and I'm sure there's enough excitement there already."

The woman nodded and left, closing the door quietly.

"Was that one of the Sisters?"

"Certainly not! We Sisters of the Good Shepherd are still wearing habits. That is one of the lay women who help out here. Now, Father, let's get down to business. You must contact the Davis family and explain to them the necessary procedures regarding Pam's official admittance."

Joe dialed the Davis home and waited. After explaining the latest developments regarding their daughter and filling them in about the red tape that had to be cleared up, Mrs. Davis asked him to hold the line until her husband listened in on the extension phone. "Sister, could you do the same? You could answer their questions better than I."

"Good idea, Father."

Within minutes there was a four-way conversation going on, but with Mrs. Davis doing most of the talking. "I am so upset over this whole thing, but I don't see why Pam should stay there. After all, there's no pregnancy to contend with now. *(She sounds relieved. She's more concerned about her image than her daughter's problems.)* And besides, isn't Good Shepherd Home a place for 'bad' girls?"

Father Joe didn't have a chance to respond. "We have no bad girls, as you put it, Mrs. Davis . . . just girls who have been hurt, in one way or another. Your daughter will not be living in a jail. She will be living in a home where everyone works together as a family. She will have recreation, education, work, but most of all — love." The mother superior's voice sounded quite defensive and her face was red. *(She must have a temper too! That's telling the old girl, Mother Bernadette.)*

"Sister, I will handle all the things you've outlined. Thank you for showing an interest in Pam. My wife and I are most grateful and we will see you tomorrow afternoon. Thank you," Mr. Davis said impatiently. *(His wife must be getting on his nerves too. About time the old boy spoke up.)*

The intercom began to buzz again; this time it was Doctor Russell. "Tell the Father that Pam is all right. Whoever did the job apparently knew what he was doing. Her blood count is low and we'll have to build her up with a lot of iron. She's apparently lost a lot of blood, far more than she could spare. I'm certain this is an illegal abortion, so I'll have to contact the authorities. Pam said she would cooperate, so we'll let them take it from there. Right now, I think the best thing for the girl is rest and a warm meal."

"Well, it looks like your little girl will be fine, Father," the mother superior said, smiling again.

"I'm sure she will . . . and thank you." Joe started for the door, then stopped. "Tell me, Sister, just out of curiosity . . . do you and the Sisters have trouble relating to the girls?"

The nun looked at him, puzzled. She held the heart-shaped emblem which hung from the neck of her white habit and thought a moment before she answered: "Why should we? We just do our job and let God handle the rest."

"Any calls, Dearie?" Joe asked as he entered the rectory.

"None to worry about. Look what just came!" Dearie was beaming as she waved a telegram.

Joe read it quickly. "No wonder you're so excited. Johnny's coming home tomorrow."

"Just think, Father Joe, it's been five years since I've seen my boy. I can hardly wait . . . I know I won't sleep tonight."

"He could stay here, if you like, Dearie. There's the guest room and it will give you time to be with him."

"Oh could he, Father? It would be such a joy to have him here and cook his favorites again."

"Sure, get it ready. One of us will take you to the airport to pick him up after Mass. I may have enough time to make it to the bishop's office by noon." The last phrase brought with it a feeling of anxiety again.

"Land sakes, I was so excited . . . I forgot to tell you about Father Rahner. The chancery called right after you left and Father George had to go down to talk to the vicar-general. The poor boy looked worried when he left."

Joe went to his room to wash up before dinner. "Don't forget the wedding rehearsal at 6:30," Dearie called after him. *(The wedding rehearsal . . . I forgot all about it! I was hoping to talk with George. I never should have blown up at him like that this morning. God knows he's got enough problems without my adding to them.)*

George still hadn't returned when dinner was over. "I'll put his dinner in the oven to keep it warm. You don't suppose he's been with the vicar-general all this time, do you?" Dearie showed concern.

"I doubt it, but if he does come in while I'm at church, ask him to stop over, okay?" Joe asked as he poured himself another cup of coffee.

"How's your nice friend . . . Father Pieri?" Father Benetti asked out of the blue.

"Fine. He's making a retreat right now." Joe couldn't understand the sudden interest in his friend.

"I'll bet he doesn't go for all this new stuff . . . these demonstrations and nuns running around in lay clothes, does he?"

"I haven't really spoken to him about it," Joe answered. He tried hard not to carry this conversation any further. Father Benetti was so certain that Ed was solid in his vocation, Joe wouldn't dare disillusion him. That would be more than the old man could bear if he were to be aware that the one priest of the "new breed" that he was sure of, was thinking about leaving the priesthood.

"Now, there's a fine young priest," Benetti continued. "Has his feet on the ground; but you see, that's because he takes time to be alone with Christ. Didn't he go on retreat with you just a few months ago?"

"As a matter of fact, he did."

"Good. Good. He knows the value of prayer. Some of these new ones should take a lesson from Father Pieri . . . a fine young man."

"Father Joe, the wedding party is arriving at the church . . . and look at what they're wearing!" Dearie screamed as she leaned over the sink on tiptoes to peer out the kitchen window.

Walking up the path to the church were four young women and their escorts. Father Benetti stood beside Mrs. Quinlan and he also went on tiptoes. "My God! What are they wearing?" he shouted as he caught the view.

"Hot pants, Father," Dearie answered simply.

"Hot 'what'?"

"Hot pants. In my day we called them 'shorts.' "

"In my day we called them *indecent!* They're not going into the church dressed like that, are they?" Benetti questioned, then added, "At least one of them is dressed fairly decently . . . but I still don't like slacks on women in church."

"Which one are you talking about?" Mrs. Quinlan strained to see.

"The tallest one . . . with the long brown hair. See her standing next to the blond girl?"

Mrs. Quinlan turned from the window and began to laugh hysterically.

"What's so funny?" the old priest asked.

"That's the groom, Father. Wait till *she* turns around."

"I've lived too long . . ." he mumbled, then went to the den to watch the news.

Joe went directly to the front of the altar and began giving the wedding party a few instructions about where they were to take their place at the altar. Rosemary Stanton, the bride, introduced her fiancé to Joe. *(How could a cute kid like Rosemary come up with such a character? She could have done better than that. He might not look so bad if he'd shave that facial fungus off.)* Joe stared at the young man's long beard. *(He looks like Jesus Christ . . . oh, and here comes John the Baptist.)* The best man, also bearded, took his place next to the groom.

"Before we go any further, Father . . . let me remind you that the rehearsal dinner will be at Jacques' Steak House right after we leave here," the groom said. "I'm looking forward to talking with you. Rosemary's told me so much about you."

Joe looked at Rosemary in her pale-green, well-filled sweater and hot pants. *(I wonder what she's told him about me? I don't even know her that well.)* Realizing that he was succumbing to male vanity, he cleared his throat and continued the rehearsal.

Joe promised the prospective bride and groom that he would meet them later at the rehearsal dinner, then rushed to the rectory when he saw George's car in the drive.

"They're at it again, Father Joe," Dearie motioned towards the den where heated voices were emerging.

"Now what?" Joe said disgustedly.

When Joe entered the room George was leaning over Father Benetti with his arms outstretched. "For God's sake, Father, I was only teasing. It was only a joke."

"I'm not stupid. I knew those weren't nuns dressed in hot pants; but how do you explain the sacrilege of even inferring that nuns would dress that way? What kind of priest are you?" Benetti asked angrily.

"Wait a minute, Benetti. I'm not about to defend my priesthood to you or anybody else. I told that to the vicar-general this afternoon and I'll say it again: What gives you the right to judge me?"

Benetti didn't answer. He just groaned in a disgusted manner and opened his breviary.

"Answer me!" George said demandingly, then turned to Joe. "Did you ever see a guy pray so much? . . . and do so little?"

"Calm down, George . . . listen to me . . ." Joe took his arm but George pulled away.

"No, damn it! I want to have my say too!"

"Do you ever pray?" Benetti asked simply.

"I don't take twelve hours a day to read some mumbo jumbo . . . 'reading my Office' as you call it." George's voice was still tinged with anger.

"How do you know what the Office is? I've never seen you with the breviary since you got here!" Benetti screamed back.

"And you never will! You think God is going to send you to hell, if there is such a place, for missing your daily Office? Doesn't working for the good of my fellowman count for anything? Why do you guys spend all day asking God to do the things you should be doing yourselves? God isn't going to change the world . . . He wants man to do it!" George was flushed with temper. "And let me tell you something else . . ." He began to wave his finger at the old priest. "You may not like it, but I'm just as much a priest as you. In fact, I think I am *more* of a priest than you!"

Father Benetti stood, slammed his breviary shut and bawled back, "Heretic! Why don't you start your own religion? You're so worried about pollution, air pollution, water pollution ... why aren't you worried about 'Catholic Church pollution'? You know why? Because you are its main pollutant!" Father Benetti started for the door that led to the hall.

"That's right! Run off and prepare one of those inspiring sermons of yours about hell and purgatory! Or how about indulgences? That's always a grabber!" George yelled.

Benetti stopped at the doorway and looked over his shoulder at George. His voice was unusually calm. "In your sermons, Father, you keep talking about love — love the blacks ... love the poor. When are you going to love those who differ with you regarding theology? When are you going to really love?" Benetti walked away.

George stood motionless in the middle of the room. Joe remained silent. George flopped in a chair, saying, "Maybe the old man's right ... maybe I let go because he asked the same question I've been asking myself for some time: *What kind of priest am I?*"

"George, you've been under pressure the past few days. All this will blow over," Joe sympathized. "I know I didn't help things for you this morning when I sounded off — "

"Forget it," the younger priest waved his hand listlessly. "I've learned one thing today from talking to you this morning, Benetti tonight, and the vicar-general this afternoon. The problem in the Church today is not that the priests aren't relating to the people. How can we? ... when we can't even relate to each other?"

Joe made a quick call to check in with Monsignor Flannagan before he left for the rehearsal party. His pastor seemed to be in unusually good spirits. He made Joe promise not to worry about visiting him for a few days since St. Monica's seemed to need him more than he. Joe was surprised by how philosophically the monsignor accepted the news about his nuns wearing lay clothes; he also expressed sympathy for George's dilemma and the T.V. interview. Before he said good-bye, the monsignor managed a slight laugh and said, "All these troubles lose some of their importance when a man knows he's about to meet his Master."

The wedding party and a few guests were already seated when Joe arrived at the restaurant. "Sit here, Father; we saved you a chair at the main table." The groom stood to pull out the chair for Joe. On Joe's right was one of the bridesmaids, a very curvy young thing who giggled, "Oh, I never sat next to a priest before! I'm not Catholic, you know."

Joe took his chair uncomfortably as the girl began to babble on and on about some of her Catholic friends and how she used to attend "services" with them in their church. "Up and down, up and down . . . I thought I was at a physical fitness class or something." Joe smiled cordially. "Tell me, Father, don't you think Frank would have made a good priest . . . he's so smart and talks so good about almost everything." She pointed to the groom. "He was in the seminary, you know."

Joe looked to his left at the bearded long-haired groom. "No, I didn't know."

"She's right, Father. I was only two years away from ordination, then I left, continued my education and now I'll receive my Ph.D. next spring. I'm in education administration." *(Wow, was I wrong about him! His looks certainly deceived me. When I first met him, I wouldn't even have given him credit for holding a job. I must be getting more like Benetti every day.)*

As Frank continued talking, the bridesmaid kept edging closer and closer in to hear what he was saying. *(I wish she would move . . . or Frank talk louder.)* Joe squirmed uncomfortably in his chair to avoid touching the girl. In her most unpolished manner the girl asked, "Well, if you thought the seminary was so great, how come you didn't stay and be a priest?"

"Many personal reasons. I suppose celibacy was one of the most important factors that ultimately made me alter my plans," Frank stated honestly.

"You mean not being able to get married and go out with

girls and stuff?" She could hardly wait for his confirmation.

Frank nodded. "And having children . . . I love kids. I hope Rosemary and I can have a large family. Thank God, I've found a girl who shares my feeling." He reached for Rosemary's hand and squeezed it tightly.

"Well," the bridesmaid said as she chomped on a breadstick, "I'm not too sure I think not getting married or having girl friends is a good idea." She looked directly at Joe. "It's not natural!"

"You're right," Joe answered. "It's *supernatural* and without God's help, I doubt if I could do it!" At the expense of crowding the groom, Joe moved his chair closer to him to avoid her body against him.

Joe excused himself early from the rehearsal party when he finally became fed up with answering a thousand questions about the new liturgy, birth control, draft dodgers, abortion, papal infallibility, etc. He felt as if he were conducting a catechetic session and always, he had to be aware to say the right thing for Joe was certain he would be quoted. One phrase pertaining to any of these subjects taken out of context could create a completely different picture than the one he had tried to paint. When Joe sat behind the wheel and removed his jacket and collar, it seemed as though he were temporarily relieving himself of all obligations that went with that little white band. *(Just once I would like to relax over dinner with laymen and feel that I wasn't being interviewed. I hate explaining doctrine and the Church's views on social problems to a group of faces sipping martinis. Right away everybody is an authority when they probably haven't read a Catholic periodical in years. What is it in booze that makes every male guest suddenly remember their days when they were altar boys serving Mass for "good old Father so and so"? Tonight, I'm going to kick off my shoes, relax . . . and if I hear the words "conservative" or "liberal" one more time . . .)*

Joe turned the station to some soft music. *(That's more like it. I wonder if we had any calls about the change in the nuns' dress. I can hear George now . . . George, I wonder how he would have handled that bridesmaid back there. Bold little thing, she was ... cute though ... too cute for comfort. Wonder if she was just playing dumb? No, she wasn't really too informed about the Church, or anything else, for that matter. But maybe she was trying to trap me into saying something she could turn around. It was obvious she liked the attention from the rest of the guys there ... and she was sure giving me plenty of attention. There goes my male pride again ...)*

Joe spied the silhouettes of two figures in the den when he pulled into the rectory drive; they seemed to be engrossed in deep conversation. Rather than take the risk of walking into another Benetti vs. George scene, he headed for the darkened church. *(Wonder what some of my "reporting" parishioners would say if they saw me going into the church at 10 p.m. Would they be as eager to report that to their neighbors as they are everything else? But from the way they twisted my actions this past week, it would probably wind up with me sneaking into the church to confiscate the Blessed Sacrament for a "Black Mass.")*

Joe looked at the large red sanctuary lamp burning alone at the altar and remembered how a few years back it was complemented by all the small dancing flames of the candles burning at the side altars. He suddenly realized how much he missed those little candles. As a child he never left a church with his family that his mother didn't light a votive candle for Aunt Mary's intention, or so that cousin Jimmy came home safe from the service, or that the neighbor next door would find a job, or even the time when she was afraid the refrigerator was about to go on the blink and they couldn't afford to get a new one. Once Joe asked his mother why people lit those little candles in front of the statues, and she explained that it was to remind this or that saint (represented by the statues) to ask God for a special favor, just as he always did when he wanted something from his Dad. It was always best to convince Mom first, then you had two people asking him instead of one. Joe knew right then and there that any candles he would ever light from then on would be in front of the statue of the Blessed Mother because Jesus had to like her better than anybody else! Now at thirty-five, he found himself kneeling before her marble image. *(Some things never change, Blessed Mother. I still need you pulling for me now as much as I did then. This was a lousy day.)*

Joe studied the face of Mary looking down at the Divine Infant in her arms. The thought of Pam's empty arms, babyless arms, trembling arms, came to his mind. His eyes wandered down the soft folds of the Blessed Mother's mantle that modestly fell to her feet, and he thought of the short skirt of the woman standing in the doorway at that cheap apartment house. He hated the picture that invaded his thoughts. *(How dare she monopolize the vision of the Perfect Woman in my mind! Why do I still sense the fragrance of the bridesmaid's cologne . . . and not the musty smell of the church? How can I look at the tender eyes of the Madonna and see the tearful eyes of Pam? And why am I kneeling here in the quiet when I should be asking George about his visit to the chancery? Why do I allow the memory of the cheapness of that woman to thwart the pure loveliness of Mary? Because tonight I can't find the priest in me, only the man. Did I come to you tonight to pray . . . or to escape?)*

Joe turned towards the tabernacle. *(Lord, I need You. I need You to remind me of what I am. I need You to remind me of what You want me to be. Give me patience, Lord. Give me humility. Help me be a good priest. Why do You make it more difficult than it already is? You sent me things today that I wasn't certain how to handle, but I managed . . . I did my job. Why do You send me temptations now?)*

"Joe! You in here?" George called from the back of the church. Joe turned, startled for a second, then stood and walked toward the center aisle in front of the altar so that George could see his figure in the darkened church. "I'm here," he answered as he genuflected and walked up the aisle.

"Had me worried . . . I heard your car come up the drive and when you didn't come in for a while, I thought I'd better check things out for myself."

"I needed to pray. It's been a busy day." Joe locked the church doors and in a voice that tried to sound not "too" anxious, he asked, "How did it go with you and the vicar-general this time?"

115

"No big deal," George answered as if he were dismissing the conversation, then changed the subject. "Do you do this often? Come over here to pray alone, I mean?"

"Whenever I think I need it." *(Why is he avoiding my question?)*

"Does it do any good?" George was grinning.

"Does *what* do any good?"

"Praying."

"Don't you believe in prayer, George?"

"I do, but not the kind of prayer where you speak and then God takes over and makes everything right. I believe that prayer is a therapy that helps us to know ourselves so that we can do something about the things that must be changed. I'm not too sure there's *Somebody* up there listening."

"You mean you don't believe that *God* is listening?" Joe asked in disbelief. "What about when you say Mass? Do you believe in the Mass? The sacraments?"

George smiled condescendingly as if Joe were a small child who still believed in Santa Claus. "I know you think of yourself as a liberal, Joe, but you really are a confused conservative. I don't want to confuse you anymore." *(Who does this kid think he is? I read as much as he does but I don't confine it to left-wing stuff . . . I've never seen him read a complete book.)*

"If you feel like that, why are you a priest, George?"

George wasn't smiling now. "Who would listen to me if I wasn't? Would you? Would the people? Everybody listens to a priest . . . and I have a lot to say!"

"And just what is that?" Joe asked as the pair stood by the rectory door.

"Look, I'm saying the same thing you are basically. I'm trying to help people to live together, love one another . . . not because they're black or white, or Catholic, Protestant, or Jew, American or Russian, rich or poor. I want to love you because you're *you*. Let's understand each other . . . make a better world."

Once in the kitchen, George took a chair and pulled another from the table for Joe, then continued, "Now I can see the benefit of prayer if people pray aloud together. If we all know each.

other's problems or hang-ups then maybe we can be of help. Take tonight for instance. If I had been with you at church tonight and heard what was bothering you, then maybe I could offer you a solution to your problem. See what I mean? Why don't you tell me what's bugging you and maybe I can offer some advice . . . maybe even a solution?".

Joe didn't answer; he thought of his present problems of temptation and wondered how George solved his own similar problems. *(Somehow I don't think your solution and mine would be the same.)* "Thanks, George, I think I already have a solution . . . a good night's sleep." *(. . . And a cold shower.)*

CHAPTER 7

SPEAK MY LANGUAGE

(Friday a.m.)

"Father Joe, the deacon is having coffee in the kitchen," Dearie beamed as she met Joe leaving his room. "He's waiting to know what you want him to do."

"I'll see him before I go over for Mass. Thanks, Dearie." Joe started to walk past her, then suddenly remembered why the smiling face. "Today's your big day. What time does John's plane arrive?"

"Eleven, Father; but don't you worry, I can make arrangements. Today's first Friday and there's sick calls."

George overheard the conversation as he was entering his room. "I'll pick him up if you like, Dearie. I don't have anything planned this morning."

"What about your classes at the university?" Joe asked, puzzled.

"No sweat, I took care of all that. I'll go to the airport," George answered sullenly, closing the door of his room behind him.

"Will you have breakfast, Father George?" Dearie called.

"Just coffee."

"What's with him?" Joe whispered.

"Don't know, Father, but he seemed kind of quiet this morning . . . not himself today."

Patrick Cooke stood when Joe entered the kitchen and outstretched his hand to introduce himself, then added eagerly, "They told me I could help out while Monsignor Flannagan's ill. I'm really looking forward to it."

Joe tried not to be too obvious as he studied the young man. Strange, even with his long hair and thick sideburns, he still looked priestly. He was well-groomed and looked quite smart in his black clerical suit and Roman collar. Joe excused himself and headed for the church, explaining that he would fill him in later after Mass.

When it came time to distribute Holy Communion, Joe was surprised when Father Benetti and Patrick came to the altar to help him; he was grateful since first Fridays swelled the attendance by at least fifty, not including the entire school.

An old lady approached Joe for Communion; she seemed to be oblivious to everything around her. She welcomed the Host with such moving devotion that Joe felt an unrest deep inside him. He recalled George's sophisticated attitude toward prayer and the sacraments which he had disclosed just the previous evening. All his books, arguments and analogies could not create a spark compared to the glow this simple old woman displayed.

By the time Joe finished the liturgy and returned to the rectory, Benetti, Patrick and George were seated at the table while Dearie bustled about, humming quietly as she served the food. Benetti and Pat were discussing the latest changes in the liturgy while George sat moodily sipping his coffee. Joe took his chair opposite George.

"Didn't take you long to get to work, Pat," Joe said as he unfolded his napkin.

"Father Benetti asked me if I wanted to help with the Communions . . . nice crowd this morning," the young man answered.

"Fine boy," Benetti said. Then looking over his spectacles, he candidly remarked, "Tell me . . . why do you young fellows insist on wearing your hair so long?"

"Not this again," George murmured disgustedly.

Patrick only laughed. "Let me put it like this, Father. I can tell by your accent that you are from Italy . . . and when you first came to this country, you had to learn to speak the language of the Americans if you wanted to communicate. Well, this is my way of speaking the language of my generation. It's communication. The kids identify with me. They know I am going to speak their language. I'm selling the same thing as you, Father, but in a different way ... a different language, that's all."

George looked on, quite pleased, then waited for Benetti's reaction. Benetti said nothing; he sat listening attentively.

Pat nonchalantly buttered his toast as he continued: "See, Father, the way I look at it ... if Fulton Sheen preached in Tokyo and his sermon was acclaimed as the greatest ever given, it better had been in Japanese, right?"

For the first time this morning, George emerged from his shell and began to applaud, exclaiming, "Bravo!" He peered at Benetti with a look that seemed to say, "Let's see what the old boy does with this one!"

Benetti leaned across the table. "Good point, son. Now try to communicate your idea to me. See if you speak *my* language too. What do you young men want to do in the Church ... where do you intend to take it?"

"We want to take it where the Holy Spirit is leading it. Most of the guys in the seminary today, including myself, are fed up with all this petty squabbling over externals. We're fed up with the arguing between conservatives and liberals. We want to bring Christ to the world and we realize there is more than one way to do it ... and more than one kind of priest to preach it."

Joe looked at George who was apparently uneasy; the look of satisfaction he had shown over Pat's first point now was traded for a serious frown. *(Does he disagree with Pat or is he searching his own motives?)* Pat paused to sip his coffee.

"Go on, I'm listening," Benetti coaxed.

"Well, I feel theology — whether it's conservative, liberal or moderate — is a necessary evil ... just like language. But sometimes like language, instead of communicating ideas and truths, it builds a barrier against itself, or sometimes it isn't learned well and is spoken badly. If I were to ask you, Father Benetti, which is the best language — Italian or American, which would you answer?"

Benetti was too smart to be trapped by the obvious knowing that Pat was aware of his heritage. "It depends on which language you speak best . . . which you understand best."

"It's the same thing with theology. Whatever brings you closer to God . . . whatever makes Christ real to you. In other words the conservative or liberal way . . . as long as it communicates some truths."

All eyes focused on Benetti as he casually lifted his cup, sipped slowly, patted his lips with his napkin and looked at George. "Today, Father Rahner, we *both* learned a lesson in communication."

George offered no sign of recognition of the old man's humble concession; he just stared into the coffee cup as he pressed his fingers firmly around the rim.

Benetti looked at the kitchen clock. "If you will excuse me, I must go. The Baxter funeral is scheduled for 9:30."

"I forgot all about the arrangements. When did the mortuary call?" Joe asked.

"Yesterday. But I knew you would be tied up this morning, so I told them I would take it." Benetti moved around the table and stood beside Pat's chair with his hand outstretched. "I hope you like your short stay at St. Monica's. It's good to see a young man with your ideals, even if you do speak a different language. One thing is the same . . . we all must speak God's language. But it's good, you know; it shows the universality of the Church . . . and the priesthood!" Benetti looked at George as he made his last remark: "Thank you for the record, Father. It was very thoughtful of you."

"What was that about?" Joe asked with bewilderment as Benetti left the room.

"Nothing, I bought the old guy a record . . . kind of a peace offering."

"That was kind, George. You bought him an Italian record?"

"No, what do I know about Italian? It was 'The Sound of Music.' Thought it would help him with his English."

Joe invited Pat to accompany him on the sick calls. When the two pulled away from the rectory, Joe asked, "Have you ever worked in a parish, Pat?"

"No, I was only ordained to the diaconate three weeks ago and this is my first assignment." Pat was excited; he was finally going to see some action after all his years of study.

"So these are your first sick calls. I'll fill you in on them before we get there. The first call will be a Mr. Jackson. He has been slowly rotting away with a terminal illness." Joe read from the sick-call book with the relevant information against the name. "I don't usually make the Communion calls. That's Monsignor Flannagan's pet project, although George took it last month. I don't know any more about these people than you do." Joe passed the book to Pat and suggested he read it aloud as Joe drove.

"Mr. Jackson ... terminal ... bedridden two years ... always goes to confession before Communion." Joe made a mental note as Pat read. *(I wonder what he has to confess? Probably scrupulous ...)* Joe dismissed the last thought as uncharitable and continued to listen as Pat read the next name.

"Mrs. Toomey ... blind ... lives with older sister ... hears well and talks a lot ... expects a blessing before you leave." *(Hope I can leave gracefully and cut the chatter today. I don't want to be pressed for time when I head for the chancery office.)*

"Linda Williams ... ten years old ... dying with leukemia ... sweet child ... likes you to tell her stories." *(Poor little Linda ... I remember giving her Holy Communion for the first time. This is going to be a rough one. I'm no good at visiting the sick any time, much less when it's a child. Thank God, Flannagan takes these calls. ... Oh, no! Who's going to take them from now on?)*

"Pat, do you know any good kids' stories?"

Pat laughed. "I'm full of stories.

"Good, you can handle little Linda ... she's a doll. Make it a happy one, will you?" Joe was about to indulge himself in the sadness of the situation when he cleared his throat and said, "Who's next?"

"Bob Winters ... Vietnam war veteran ... lost both legs ... uses wheelchair ... twenty-three years old ... married ... has small child ... wife likes to receive Communion with him." *(I didn't bring enough Hosts ... I'll break one in half. Maybe this visit is what encouraged George to get so "gung ho" on the anti-war demonstrations . . . can't blame him.)*

"Mrs. Matucek . . . Czech . . . speaks no English, only 'thank you' . . . old . . . cannot move around too well . . . always has cookies to bring to rectory." *(That's where they come from . . . thought they were homemade.)*

"Do you speak Czech, Pat?"

"Sorry, that's not my language. But don't worry; it says here that she lives with her daughter. She'll probably translate." Pat nearly dropped the book as Joe brought the car to a sudden halt.

"Keep the rest for later . . . here's our first call."

"Four down and one to go, Pat. Who's next?" Joe asked as the pair left the Matucek house carrying a box of cookies.

"Mrs. Riley."

"Do you want to stop for coffee before we make tracks for home? Still have time." Joe looked at his watch to make certain; he couldn't believe they had made such good time; it was only a little after ten o'clock.

"No need to. It says here that Mrs. Riley always has coffee and cake ready . . . and she likes to talk too." Pat smiled as he read from the book.

"What's her problem?"

"Doesn't say. It just says . . ." Pat squinted to read the small notation. "Depressive . . ." *(She should have been with us on these last few calls. She would certainly have something to be depressed about.)*

After Joe gave the middle-aged woman Holy Communion and she made her thanksgiving, she asked the two men to sit down. There was a pot of coffee and an upside-down cake waiting. "Where's that nice Father Rahner who came last time?" she asked.

"It was Father Rahner's turn last month. I'll be here this month," Joe answered as he accepted the cup. *(She doesn't look so depressed to me.)*

"Will you give him something for me?" She reached for a brightly wrapped package on the end table. "It's a scarf . . . made it myself. He can get some use from it with the weather turning chilly."

"I'll see that he gets it."

"Father Rahner was very kind to me, you know. He's even arranged to have another widow live here with me. We can kind of share the bills and it will be companionship. Ever since I lost my husband, I just never want to go anywhere or do anything; but that lady that Father brought over — she understands ... she feels the same way. One wonders why God takes those we love away from us." Joe thought of the Baxter funeral going on right now. "Well, anyway," she continued, "Father Rahner made me see that mourning and locking myself away in these rooms wouldn't make my loss any easier to bear. I'm very grateful to him." *(George isn't as unfeeling as he sometimes appears. He certainly knew how to make Mrs. Riley take a second look ... maybe I've misjudged him. I never would have thought that George could speak her language.)*

The telephone ring stopped the conversation. "Father Newman, it's for you."

George was on the other end. "Joe, I think you've got trouble. There was a kid here just a few minutes ago looking for you. He was raging on and on about you minding your own business with Pam Davis. Dearie couldn't handle him ... that's when I stepped in. This kid was really uptight. He said he was heading for Good Shepherd to talk to Pam. I hurried to call you ... figured you'd still be at Mrs. Riley's. I'm glad I caught you."

"He can't go to Good Shepherd. How did he even find out she was there?"

"From a girl friend who had talked to Mrs. Davis, I gather. Anyway, Joe, that's not important. Right now, I think you'd better hightail it over there. That kid's set on making trouble."

When the nun at the desk ushered Joe and Pat into the mother superior's office, Joe found Pam's boyfriend pounding on the desk demanding to speak with Pam. "I'm sorry that cannot be arranged," Mother Bernadette stated calmly, but emphatically. The young man turned toward Joe. "Are you Newman?"

"I'm *Father* Newman. I understand you wanted to speak to.

me." Joe tried to match Mother Bernadette's calmness but he found the task more difficult than she did.

"You the one who got Pam shut up in here?"

"I brought Pam here, yes."

"Well, you tell this lady that I want to talk to her."

"It won't do any good. Pam's not leaving with you. Haven't you done enough damage already?" Joe's voice was losing some of its previous coolness.

"Who said anything about her leaving with me? She can rot in here. I don't give a damn. But she ain't taking off and leaving me holding the bag. I gave that butcher fifty bucks and I need it back. She can get that kind of bread by just winking at her old lady. She ain't sticking me with the bill!"

"That's why you're here?" Joe asked, shocked. "To get your money for that guy who — "

"You're damn right!" the youth cut in. "Now tell this lady to let me talk to Pam."

"Get out!" Joe ordered angrily.

"Hey, man, this ain't none of your business. I got a right to get that money back. I did her a favor. How do I know that bastard was even mine?"

Joe could control himself no longer. He grabbed the front of the boy's shirt and pulled back his right hand. Mother Bernadette rose quickly. "I'm certain the authorities would be quite interested in knowing who arranged this illegal operation. Perhaps I should call them."

Joe lowered his fist and let go of the boy. He was embarrassed as Mother Bernadette advised the boy to leave immediately and opened the office door.

"You bunch of _____" the boy screamed out a litany of obscenities as he moved down the hall toward the exit.

Joe was about to apologize to the nun for the profanities rained on the trio by the young man; but before he could speak, she said as she closed the door, "Those words don't shock me, Father . ... neither does the situation. Our order has dealt with all kinds of problems, some far more distasteful than this, for the past 200 years. I appreciate your intercession, but we could have handled that young man."

125

Joe felt the same as he did when he was ten years old and Sister Mary Lois scolded him for getting in a scrape in the cloakroom. Realizing Joe's embarrassment, the mother superior changed the subject and introduced herself to Pat, then invited the two clerics to have a look around the establishment. "If you come with me, I'll take you to Sister Eileen. She can show you around, that is, if you have time."

Joe normally would have refused the invitation as the time was getting on, but when he considered his own embarrassing predicament, he looked at his watch and said, "Perhaps a short tour . . . I have an appointment at noon." *(It's almost eleven now. If I leave here in twenty minutes, drop Pat off at the rectory — and it takes fifteen minutes to get to the chancery from there — I can make it. Being punctual has never been a virtue of mine but when it's the bishop, I'd better try . . .)*

As Mother Bernadette led them down the hall to the reception desk, Joe felt more anxiety. *(Nothing like making a good impression. I made a fool of myself in front of a nun and a kid not even ordained yet . . . tremendous example, I am. Bet he thinks I'm a jerk. Good thing Mother Bernadette was there or I probably would have belted that troublemaker. Well, today I not only showed Pat what to do . . . I showed him what "not to do"!)*

The nun at the desk was crocheting rapidly before the switchboard. The headphone was pushed back on one ear and in its place was an apparatus that was hooked up to a transistor radio lying on the desk. She didn't look up as the three approached her; she was bobbing her head up and down and tapping her foot rhythmically. "Sister Eileen, I'd like you to meet . . . Sister Eileen? . . . Sister?" Mother Bernadette tapped the nun's shoulder to get her attention. She jumped up, simultaneously pulling the wire from the radio and releasing the sound of rock music through the hall. She fumbled awkwardly with the radio trying to turn down the volume and, in her frenzy, the telephone headgear slipped from her veil and fell on the desk with a bang. "Yes, Mother," she said, blushing.

"Sister Eileen, this is Father Newman and Patrick Cooke, a newly ordained deacon. Would you be kind enough to show them around? I'll get someone to relieve you."

"Glad to meet you," she said, smiling as she still fumbled with the headgear and radio.

"Sister, it's amazing how you coordinate your hearing between the radio and the phones; but do watch out that no one can hear the background," Mother grinned.

"Yes, Mother. Sorry. I was waiting for the sports news to see how the Raiders made out last night and — " She stopped when she realized she was adding fuel to the fire. She looked shyly at Joe and Pat. "I have a weakness for football too."

The tour through the Good Shepherd Home began with a look at the offices: there were case workers, social workers, psychologists, psychiatrists, M.D.'s, a dentist ... all in the main building. The next stop was the annex of classrooms. Joe kept a close eye on his watch and he was becoming more uncomfortable as the minutes ticked by. *(How do I get out of here gracefully?)*

The principal, Sister Alice, continued the tour through the high school which was one of the best-equipped schools Joe had ever seen. Besides the normal high school curriculum, everything from typing to home economics was offered. *(I have to get out of here soon or I'll be late for sure.)*

The girls were assembled in the auditorium when Joe and Pat entered. He could not see Pam. *(Suppose she's still resting.)* "I didn't realize you had so many girls," Joe whispered to the principal.

"We have eighty girls at the moment, but we try to keep the number around seventy. Would you like to visit with the girls a minute, Father?"

Before Joe could answer, he found himself being introduced. All eyes were on them, especially on Pat who, although he was twenty-three, still looked like a teen-ager himself and an exceptionally good-looking one at that. A few of the girls nudged each other, whispering and tittering. "This makes me nervous," Pat said in a barely audible voice to Joe.

"Would you care to say a few words to the girls, Father?" Sister Alice asked in a loud tone.

"Perhaps Pat can take over. I have an appointment," Joe answered.

"Thanks a lot, Father," Pat whispered again. "Do you want

127

to pick me up on your way back from the chancery? It would be rude for both of us to walk out now."

"That's just what I had in mind. You don't care, do you?"

"No, go on. I'll wait for you."

"Good luck."

"I'll need it," Pat mumbled as he turned his attention to the girls. *(Wonder how he will handle this crowd? If he can communicate with these girls, then what he told Benetti this morning will really make sense. From the looks on these girls' faces, he's already communicating.)*

Sister Alice raised her voice to be heard above the chatter. "Patrick Cooke is a deacon and will be ordained a priest later this year. Perhaps you girls would like to ask him some questions."

Several hands shot up immediately and Patrick selected his first interrogator. Joe smiled to himself. *(She's really giving him the "once over." Looks like she's found a new crush.)*

"Why do you want to be a priest?" she asked with a look that said, "What a waste." Joe looked at his watch again, then whispered to the Sister: "I'm going to slip out quietly. I have an appointment with the bishop."

"Very well, Father," she replied as she ushered him towards the exit. Outside the door, he could hear the girls giggling and he recognized a sound Joe was sure was a wolf whistle. *(Wonder what prompted that?)*

"I'm Father Joseph Newman. I have a noon appointment with the bishop." The receptionist pointed to the large clock behind her ... it was 12:15. "I'm sorry, Father Newman. We called your name a while ago. I'm afraid you'll have to wait your turn." She motioned toward the waiting room.

Joe took a vacant seat between two priests he judged to be in their late fifties. He sat down and gazed around the room. Across from him was a stout elderly priest slumped in his chair, snoring stentoriously. Joe was amused by the contrast to the figure next to him, smoking vigorously and wringing his hands. The priest on Joe's right looked right past him without even a nod and continued the conversation with the priest on Joe's left.

128

"I know just how you feel. Got the same problem at my place too. If the bishop doesn't take that rebel assistant out of my parish, he will have to find a new pastor for my church. I don't think I can take too much more."

The priest on Joe's left answered, "I feel the same way. In our day, when a pastor said something, you knew he meant business. Can't say that today."

The other priest replied, "I don't think they teach obedience in the seminary nowadays. If they do, my assistant missed all the classes. How do they think the Church survived 2,000 years?"

"Obedience and discipline. Authority was respected!"

"You're right. Obedience and discipline — that's how," the other priest repeated. *(And all the time I thought it was the Holy Spirit.)* Joe smiled silently. Then not to appear as if he too were engrossed in the conversation, he lit a cigarette.

"Father Lowell, the bishop will see you now," the secretary, a monsignor, called. The man next to the sleeping priest stubbed out his cigarette and rushed into the office. Joe seized the opportunity to sit somewhere else; he felt like an intruder to the couple who were still engaged in sympathetic criticism of their defenseless assistants.

Joe began to page through a magazine. The elderly priest's snoring grew louder until one thunderous snort finally woke him out of his deep sleep. He jumped and looked around. Joe tried not to laugh.

"Sorry. Hope I didn't disturb you, son. But that's a practice I learned early in my priesthood. Catch a few winks whenever you can . . . may not be time later." The old man smiled pleasantly at Joe.

"Father Richardson!" Joe extended his hand in surprise to the priest he had just recognized as the assistant in his old parish when he was just a child. "I'm Joe Newman. You wouldn't remember me, but I used to serve for you at St. Andrew's years ago." *(He's aged so. Not at all like I remember him when he used to stroll in the playground on lunch periods, passing out candy if you gave him the right answer out of the old Baltimore Catechism.)*

"Ah, that was years back. What brings you here, son?" the old priest asked, sitting up in his chair.

"Not too sure. The bishop sent for me."

"Aren't in any kind of trouble, are you?" The old priest pressed some fresh tobacco in his pipe.

"Not that I know of, Father," Joe answered, extending a lit match.

"That's good. Wish I was as optimistic about this meeting . . ." He paused as he cupped his hand around the match. "Thank you, son. The bishop sent for me, too. Afraid I am in trouble. Six months ago, the bishop warned me about the debt on the parish . . . said I had to raise money to pay off the mortgage. That's probably why he wants to see me today. I haven't been doing a very good job. Never was any good at raising money. How can you speak to the people about money when the parish is so hard up we have to close the school and the parishioners can hardly make enough to make ends meet? Never was any good at that."

"The worst he can do is give you a country parish and that would be great. You would have less worry and more free time," Joe tried to console.

"Or he could retire me and send me to the old priests' home," Father Richardson shook his head. "I'd hate that. I like being with the people, visiting with them and —"

"Father Richardson?" the monsignor interrupted. "The bishop will see you now."

"Good luck," Joe said as the old man rose to leave. Joe glanced toward the two priests he had sat with previously; they were still engrossed in conversation and still in total agreement. *(Shame they're not in the same parish.)*

"Joe, what are you doing here?" exclaimed a young priest two years behind Joe in the seminary. The two shook hands, then the new arrival took the seat just vacated. "Haven't seen you in years . . . still at St. Monica's, aren't you?"

The young priest's name escaped Joe momentarily and Joe was embarrassed that he couldn't return the greeting. "How have you been? Where are you now?" Joe asked, searching for the name to put with this familiar face.

"St. Margaret's, but I've got a feeling it won't be for long. That's why I came here today to ask for a transfer . . . figured I'd hit the bishop with my side of it before the pastor gets a chance. We have to reach a showdown sooner or later. So here I am. How come you're here?"

"The bishop sent for me." Joe's attention was broken by the groans of the two priests who obviously overheard his friend's conversation.

"Hey, Stan, how's it going?" another young priest greeted as he approached the pair. *(That's it! Stan Koscka.)* The young intruder nodded to Joe, then excused himself and continued on his way.

"Stan, do you think you'll get the transfer?" Joe was anxious to acknowledge his friend's name.

"I'd better get the transfer, or I'm asking for a year's leave of absence. Joe, you wouldn't believe the setup I'm in. Here I am thirty-three years old, been ordained for almost eight years, and I have a Master's in Philosophy, in charge of 130 students in my teaching at the seminary, yet in my own parish, I'm treated on the same level as an altar boy. I must ask permission to leave the rectory and keep a number where I can be reached. He wants me in by eleven every night and I have to give him a rundown on everything I do. I've got news for you — I didn't get ordained to be some pastor's errand boy. This is for the birds and I've had it. He keeps screaming about obedience like I was one of the kids in the grade school. I feel like I have to have permission to go to the john!" Stan's voice was bitter and much louder than Joe wished; he could see the two old pastors across the room staring at Stan and nudging each other.

"Maybe things will work out for you, Stan. All you can do is try," Joe replied in a very low tone, hoping he would take the hint.

"Get this!" Stan said, motioning toward the secretary's desk. There stood a tall slender young man in blue jeans and a Roman collar that was barely visible under a long beard; his hair hung loosely around his shoulders, and around his neck he wore a gold chain on which hung a peace symbol. "I don't believe it," Joe said, stunned.

131

"Maybe he thinks he's the Messiah. Get a load of those shoes," Stan nodded as Joe turned his gaze to the young man's feet. He was wearing a pair of leather sandals and his feet were quite dirty. It was comical to watch the receptionist try not to show shock when she asked him if he had an appointment. Apparently she said the wrong thing. The hippie type began to wave his arms and bawl, "Have I got an appointment? I've been trying to get an appointment and no one will see me! I demand to see the bishop! Either he gives me and my colleagues an interview or I'll call the press and T.V. He knows why I'm here. When are we going to talk to him about getting our faculties in this diocese? I'm fed up with waiting for the 'institutional Church' to reach their decision. Now either I get in there and talk with him or he'll have more people to talk with than me. Wait till the newspapermen come with me — because that's who I'll bring the next time. We want action and we want it now!"

"I hope the bishop gives him his faculties and assigns him to my pastor," Stan laughed. "And the old man thinks I'm way out. He should see this!"

Joe looked at the two older priests again. The one on the left was pointing to the newcomer. "See what I mean? Is this what it's coming to?"

The desk clerk called for the vice-chancellor who ordered the mod cleric to leave. As he made his way to the door he kept shouting his threats about bringing media representatives on his next visit. He thrust the door open and stormed out, almost colliding with Ed Pieri in the open doorway who stood gaping in shock. The hippie priest walked around him, brushing his shoulder as he passed. Joe jumped from his chair and rushed to Ed. "What are you doing here?"

"What was that?" Ed asked, jerking his head toward the priest still waving his arms as he walked down the hall, then realized that Joe was standing before him and added, "What are *you* doing here?"

"I'll explain later," Joe said quietly. "Come over here and sit down." Joe led Ed to a chair; he wanted to ask him a thousand questions, but the door to the office opened again. "Father Newman? The bishop will see you now!"

132

CHAPTER 8

THE GOOD SHEPHERD

(Friday afternoon)

"Take a seat, Joseph," the bishop said, pointing to the leather chair opposite his desk. Joe hesitated as to whether he should kiss his ring, but the bishop didn't indicate that he was expecting it, so Joe obeyed and sat in the easy chair. All the tension he had stifled earlier seemed to erupt; Joe realized his hands were perspiring. He was about to offer a greeting when the telephone rang. "Excuse me, I think this is the call I've been waiting for." The bishop reached for one of the two phones on his desk. *(Must be his private number.)*

"Do you want me to wait outside?" *(Say "yes" so I can find out what Ed's doing here.)*

"No, this will just take a minute." *(I don't know why I'm so worried about what Ed's here for, when I don't even know why I'm here . . .)* Joe looked around the room in an attempt to appear as if he were not listening to the conversation. *(Wonder who he's talking to. Probably somebody important. I can tell by the tone of his voice . . . sounds so professional.)*

After a series of "yes's" and "good's," the bishop said, "That's good news, and I don't have to tell you how much I appreciate your pushing for this bill. These foster homes are so important for these delinquent kids . . . Then you'll call me as soon as you hear . . ." A pause, then, "Thanks again. Good-bye." *(Must be the state legislature and one of the representatives is calling him to let him know how it's going.)*

The bishop sat back in his chair and folded his arms. "Joseph, the reason I sent for you — " The phone rang again. "Sorry," the bishop said, reaching for the other telephone. "Yes, this is Bishop Condry . . . I plan to be there . . . You can expect the usual complaints . . . Well, make a note of it and I'll try to cover that topic in my talk to the Priests' Council, and if anything else comes up, let me know . . . Bye." He hung up the phone and pressed the intercom at the same time. "This will just take a second." The voice answered from the other end of the intercom. "Yes, Bishop." *(That's his secretary . . . the monsignor who showed me in here.)*

"Send in my lunch, will you, Charlie?" *(Charlie! He looks anything but a "Charlie" . . . a lot stuffier than the bishop himself.)*

"You don't mind, do you? I didn't even take breakfast this morning . . . didn't have time. Now as I was saying about why I called you here today. Excuse me again," the bishop said as he rose from his chair and adjusted the venetian blind to keep the sun from shining directly on his desk. "Can't stand the glare," he explained as he took his seat again. The door opened and in walked Charlie, carrying a tray. There was only a simple sandwich and a small pot of coffee. The bishop thanked him as he left the room. "I never eat much for lunch, but I'm a great snacker." He opened a side desk drawer and pulled out three bags of candy . . . all chocolate. "There are chocolate-covered almonds, peanuts and raisins . . . would you like some?"

"No, thank you," Joe smiled. *(I can't get over how "human" he is . . . he has a sweet tooth too.)* Joe finally began to relax.

The bishop poured his coffee; Joe smiled when he watched him empty the contents of artificial sweetener in it. The bishop held up the empty pack. "I think they're trying to tell me something out there. They want me to cut down on my sugar.

"Were you out there just now when that commotion took place?" the bishop asked.

"You mean the priest shouting about getting faculties in this diocese?"

The bishop nodded affirmatively. "I expect him to make a few waves before it's all over, but I can't hand out faculties to newcomers in this diocese like they were calling cards. I have all I can do to keep my own priests happy . . . well, reasonably happy, that is," the bishop smiled.

"How are you making out while Monsignor Flannagan's gone?"

"We've had a few little upsets . . . but nothing I can't handle," Joe answered. *(I wish he would get to the point.)*

"You speaking about the other assistant, Father Rahner? That young man has a lot of zeal, as long as he channels it in the right direction."

Joe remained silent; he was hoping he wouldn't be called upon to make an evaluation of George. The bishop continued: "I spoke with Monsignor Flannagan on the phone yesterday. He won't be coming back to St. Monica's. I think you're aware of that, aren't you?" Joe nodded. "It's too bad about his condition. Flannagan's a fine priest . . . made a fine pastor, too."

"Yes, Bishop. I never realized just how much he did until this past week. St. Monica's is a big parish and there are many demands."

"That's what I want to talk to you about, Joseph. Being a pastor of a big parish isn't an easy job. Were you aware that a letter was sent to me concerning you . . . also a phone call?" *(Old lady Ferris, I'll bet, or one of her busybody friends. God, he must know all about the rumors . . . here it comes!)*

"I'm not surprised . . . but if you'll let me explain," Joe began. For the next ten minutes, he filled the bishop in about his meeting with Mrs. Ferris and the rumors about his being seen with a girl when in fact it was Gregg Bruno. Joe also mentioned the episode in the parking lot when he had finished anointing Tom Baxter. Upon concluding, Joe waited for the bishop to reply, but was puzzled and a little worried as the bishop just kept staring and frowning.

Finally, he spoke. "Gregg Bruno . . . Bruno. . . . Where have I heard that name?" The bishop was searching his memory. Suddenly, with a look of surprise, the bishop jumped from his chair and walked toward a small table in the corner of the room. "Here it is! I knew I remembered the name," he said, picking up a newspaper and handing it to Joe. "This must be your fellow," the bishop said as he pointed to a story at the bottom of the page. The headline read: "One Teen-ager Acquitted; Another Sentenced to Ten Years on Narcotics Charge." Joe was so eager to find out which of the two was Gregg, that he began to read, completely oblivious of the bishop's presence. He was relieved to learn Gregg had been the one acquitted, but puzzled why Gregg had not told him about the date of the trial when he had just spoken to him a few days ago on the telephone.

"Your young man was lucky," the bishop stated as he took the paper from Joe. "Shame that Baxter boy didn't get off the stuff before he had the fatal accident . . ." The bishop took his chair again. "Well, let's get back to the real reason I sent for you today." *(The "real reason"? I thought that was it. Now what?)*

"As I said before, Monsignor Flannagan will not be returning to St. Monica's. I would like to appoint you as pastor. What do you think?" *(Me! . . . the pastor!)*

"If you think I can handle the job." *(I don't believe it . . . me, the pastor!)*

"I think you can handle it. Monsignor Flannagan thinks you can handle it, but what's more important is: do *you* think you can handle it?"

"Yes," Joe stated simply. *(I should have said, "Yes, I hope so . . .")*

"Then it's settled. The announcement will come out formally in next week's Archdiocesan News." Bishop Condry looked at his watch. "I'm running behind schedule today." He rose from his chair as if to conclude the interview. Joe was about to speak when the bishop interrupted him. "About the letter and phone call . . . you were innocent of the charges against you. However, let it be a lesson in prudence . . . also a lesson of how all of us misjudge each other."

"Yes, Bishop . . . and thank you." Joe reached out his hand.

"Good luck with St. Monica's . . . and let's pray that Monsignor Flannagan won't have to suffer. He's a good man . . . always been a good man . . ."

"You were in there long enough . . . now tell me why you're here. You're the last person I expected to see in here today," Ed

Pieri said after Joe came out of the bishop's private office.

"When did you get back from the retreat house? And how come you're here?" Joe asked excitedly, ignoring his friend's inquiry.

"I just left there because I had this appointment, and —"

"Father Pieri? The vicar-general will see you now . . ." the secretary called.

"Listen, I've got to go in," Ed said quickly. "Can you wait for me?"

"I promised this deacon I would pick him up right after my appointment. Can you meet me at my place as soon as you finish here?"

"Sure thing. I have a lot to tell you. But first, hurry, what did you come here for today?" Ed asked, as he began walking away.

"Father Pieri? The vicar-general will see you now . . ." the secretary called.

"I was just appointed pastor of St. Monica's," Joe answered dumbfoundedly.

"*What?*" Ed called back as the secretary closed the door behind him.

It was a toss-up. Which did Joe feel more as he drove back to the Good Shepherd home — shock, or anxiety? Shock, because he still couldn't believe he was the pastor . . . anxiety, because he still hadn't talked to his best friend. *(What was he doing there? Is he really going to ask to leave? But he looked more at peace than he did before he left for the retreat house . . . or was I just seeing something there that wasn't there at all? Maybe I just wanted to believe these few days of getting away to pray would change him. I hope Pat's waiting for me so we can leave right away and I can finally talk to Ed . . .)*

"Father Newman, your friend is waiting for you . . . they asked me to send you to the kitchen," Sister Eileen said as she pulled the earplug away. *(Why the kitchen? As if I have all the time in the world . . .)*

Sister Eileen stopped two girls as they passed in the hall.

"Will you take Father Newman to the kitchen, please?" Sister Eileen smiled sweetly and replaced the earplug to the transistor.

"Did you ever get the score from the game last night?" Joe asked.

"Six to four . . . Raiders," was her simple answer.

Joe was amused at the Sister's casual manner as he walked away with the two girls who led him down the hall, then through a door that brought him to a huge courtyard. "The kitchen's right down this path, and through that door, Father," one of them pointed out.

Halfway across the path, Joe turned, startled as a golf caddy cart tooting away came up alongside them. On the back of the cart read a sign: "Polish Power." The driver, a nun, waved as she passed them. "Hi, Father, girls!"

"That's Sister Sylvia. She's taking the supplies for the evening meals to our cottages," one of the girls explained.

In the center of the landscape was a tremendous bed of flowers. "It's late in the year for such large blooms, isn't it?" Joe asked.

"Not for us, Father. The Sisters of the Cross sprinkle them with holy water!"

"Oh," Joe answered stupidly. *(What faith! Who are the Sisters of the Cross?)*

"Here we are, Father," the taller of the two girls said as she opened the door to the kitchen. There at a huge wooden table stood Pat with his sleeves rolled up and wearing a butcher's apron. His arms were white from fingertips to elbows as he struggled laboriously with a gigantic mound of dough, kneading back and forth as if he were handling the oars on a huge galleon. "How much longer on this, Sister?" he asked.

"Keep it up a little longer, dear." The pleasant middle-aged nun laughed happily as she sprinkled more flour over the dough. "I'll grease the tins, then we can form the loaves."

"Yes, Sister," Pat answered. He seemed to be working up a sweat. "Do you do this often?"

"Whenever we have a surplus of various ingredients. You should visit when we get berries — far messier." The nun gave out another hearty laugh and Pat laughed right along with her.

"See they put you to work," Joe intruded.

"Ah, looks like I'm going to lose my helper. You can wash up over here, Patrick." The jolly nun untied Pat's apron as he lifted his arms as if he were ready for surgery.

"Father, this is Sister Martha . . . and she's a slave driver." Pat winked as the nun shook hands with Joe.

"Glad to meet you, Father." She turned back to Pat. "You can't leave without tasting the bread." Sister Martha dug into the dough, took out a small section and began kneading it with her very experienced hands. "It's not as easy as it looks," Joe said softly. She shaped it into a small loaf, placed it in a tin, greased the top quickly, then covered it with a warm damp cloth.

"Here, Patrick . . . when you get back to the rectory, you can bake it youself. Try to keep it at room temperature until it rises, then just pop it in the oven . . . about 450 degrees . . . you'll know when it's done by the nice brown color. Actually, the reason I'm sending this home with you is so that you'll have a reason to come back, to return my tin and cloth. I get more help in my kitchen this way." She laughed again.

"Thanks, Sister," Pat hugged Sister Martha affectionately with one arm as he balanced the tin with the other. "But you didn't have to give me an excuse to come back . . . you'll be seeing plenty of me."

"You boys will have coffee before you leave," she said, already heading for the stove. "And you must have just a taste of my peach pie." She reached for two dishes and set them on the tray.

"Looks like we're staying a while longer, Father. She doesn't take 'no' for an answer. Isn't she a doll?" Pat whispered.

Joe looked at his watch. *(I can't be rude to these Sisters a second time today . . . besides I haven't even had lunch. Hope Ed doesn't mind my being just a few minutes late.)*

Joe and Pat finished their refreshments, thanked Sister Martha and headed back towards the main building. "Aren't they all just great? I love this place," Pat stated enthusiastically, still carrying his bread.

"Shhh! What's that?" Joe strained to hear. From the chapel on one side of the large courtyard came the sound of chanting.

"That's the Sisters of the Cross. Sister Martha told me all about them, then took me over to see them in the chapel after lunch. Come on, let's go in," Pat said as he turned to cross the yard. *(Sisters of the Cross . . . oh yeah, they're the ones with the "holy water.")* Joe stepped around a small section of flowers, then looked back to admire them.

"Would you please tell me about these Sisters of the Cross?" Joe asked curiously.

"They're girls who were sent here to the Sisters like the rest of the kids we saw today; only they stayed and became nuns . . . contemplative ones at that!" Pat held the door closed a second to give him more time to explain. "They used to be called the 'Magadalens' and they wore the brown habit of the Carmelites; but since the Vatican renewal, they now wear the white habit of the Good Shepherd Sisters and they've changed their name to 'Sisters of the Cross.' "

Joe was startled to see so many nuns, at least forty of them, all dressed in the white habit and black veil; the only distinguishing feature from the Sisters of the Good Shepherd were the silver crosses that hung from their necks instead of the silver hearts. He took a place in one of the pews and knelt to pray as the chanting of the Sisters echoed through the chapel. *(It's easy to pray in here . . . it's like another world, Lord.)* Joe looked up at the large statue of Christ with the sheep on his shoulders. "I am the Good Shepherd; I know my sheep and they know me." *(These Sisters really have to know their "sheep" too. How well do I know mine? I had to use a book to tell me the problems of the sick calls I made this morning. Those are my sheep. I'm their pastor now. God, I don't know if I'm going to be any good at it. I followed the example of the Good Shepherd this week, Lord. Remember? "Leave the ninety-nine in the desert and go after the one which is lost . . ." Well, I did that. I went out and looked for Pam. She was lost.)*

Joe pictured in his mind the image of the wounded sheep being bound up by Christ. *(Pam was wounded physically; but more, emotionally . . . and now these Sisters are going to "bind" up the wounds.)* His meditation was broken by the soft chimes of a clock. *(Ed's waiting for me. Lord, give him the same boost You just gave me. Make him realize why we became priests . . . what it's all about. I know I'm still learning and I have a long way to go. Ed's searching so hard right now . . . help him out, will You?)*

There was a slight chill in the air as Joe and Pat entered the car. After they drove a few blocks, Pat stopped long enough from his praises of the Sisters and asked, "Do you think you could turn on the heater? It's a little chilly in here."

"Sure. You cold?" Joe reached for the switch.

"No, but Sister Martha did say 'room temperature'!" Pat tucked the damp cloth under the tin gently as he looked at his treasure that lay between the two of them . . . his homemade bread.

Joe began to laugh, but when he realized how much the bread really meant to Pat and just how serious he was, he tried to cover up by asking, "How did your talk with the girls go?"

"A little rough at first. They asked me why I'd chosen the priesthood; but I don't think they were really interested. So I just listened to them for a while, then finally we started to communicate. Hey, did you meet Sister Sylvia? She's something else! Funniest person I ever met, but she can turn around and be as strict as she has to. The girls really love her too. Just goes to show you, Father; you can relate even if you're wearing a habit!" Pat sounded as if he had just made an important discovery. *(This kid has zeal. He'll make a good priest. It's great to know we have priests like him for tomorrow's generation. Man, I sound like I'm really getting old!)*

Joe found himself in a peculiar position as he played host back at the rectory; he didn't wish to dampen Dearie's enthusiasm by telling her that he was the new pastor for that would mean telling her how ill Monsignor Flannagan really was. Neither did he really want to sit and make small talk with Father John Quinlan when he was dying to get Ed off to the side to find out his decision.

"Coming home this soon was a surprise to me as well as to my mother, but this is not strictly a vacation. Actually, I'm here to recruit priests for the missions from this diocese; the need is great. Also, I will probably speak at a few parishes to help raise money. You can't imagine the poverty! I'm sorry Monsignor Flannagan is ill — I was hoping to get his permission to speak here at St. Monica's," Father Quinlan informed. "Do you think perhaps you will be talking to him? I also want to make certain he doesn't mind my using the guest room like this."

(Now is as good a time as any . . .) "The guest room is yours for as long as you need it. And you're welcome to speak at St. Monica's any time you wish." Joe realized everyone was looking at him strangely, as if they were wondering, "Who gave him the authority?" All, except Ed. He was grinning but looking down so as not to give away the fact that he was in on the news. Joe leaned forward in his chair. "This will probably come as a shock to you . . . it certainly was a shock to me. But the reason I was called to see the bishop today was . . . well, he appointed me the new pastor." Joe was almost stammering and he felt self-conscious as Father Benetti, the first to acknowledge Joe's announcement, rose from his chair to congratulate him. Ed in turn shook his hand, simultaneously jabbing his arm, and saying, "You old son of a gun . . . my buddy, 'the pastor'!" George raised his hand limply and smiled, almost sardonically, "Well, how does it feel to be a full-fledged member of 'the establishment'?"

(What's bugging him?) "I became that when I was ordained. So did you." *(That sounded sarcastic. I shouldn't have even answered that rhetorical question. That's it! Right off the bat, I'm putting a wedge between me and my assistant. God, give me patience!)*

Dearie gave Joe a gentle hug. "Congratulations, Father Joe. I wish you the very best." Her eyes began to fill with tears. "Forgive me, I'm such a silly old lady." Joe recognized the tears were not those of joy but of sadness. He knew Dearie understood this appointment meant that Monsignor Flannagan wouldn't be returning, and the two had been friends for so many years. Joe tried to comfort her.

"Dearie, you know Monsignor Flannagan wouldn't want any tears on a day that you've been waiting for so long. John didn't travel all this way to find you all teary — "

"And besides, we have two things to celebrate now," John

interrupted as he shook Joe's hand. "I was telling George and Ed before you came home that a few priest friends of mine planned a little get-together . . . kind of a welcome home party for me tonight. One of my friends has a father who owns a restaurant and he's offered to let us have a private room complete with cocktails and buffet, and all of you are invited."

Father Benetti thanked John for the invitation but declined, explaining that he should have an early night since he still had the six o'clock Mass. Dearie said that she felt this should be a night out just for the boys to enjoy themselves without "fussing over a whining old lady."

"I'm in!" Ed accepted.

Joe looked at Pat, "What about you? You won't feel too badly if we save your bread for breakfast, will you?" he teased. He turned to ask George but discovered he had already left the room. "Is George coming?"

"He'll have to now . . . can't say 'no' to his pastor," John laughed. "I'll just call Gene and let him know we'll all be there at eight." John went to the phone.

Patrick and Dearie headed for the kitchen as she explained the baking instructions all over again while Benetti excused himself to go to his room. Joe seized the first opportunity he had to see Ed alone. "Let's go to my office," he said, pulling at Ed's arm.

"Okay, we can talk. Now fill me in on what happened with the retreat," Joe said anxiously.

"You should have been there! It was great! The retreat master was something else . . . you wouldn't believe this guy's story," Ed rattled on excitedly. "Let me tell you about this guy. He's a religious order priest, about our age . . . brilliant, has a double doctorate and teaches biochemistry at the university. Dynamic man . . . wish you could meet him."

Joe tried not to interrupt Ed; he knew enough about him to know that you just had to sit back and wait for him to finish his story. *(Go on . . . go on. Who cares about him? What's with you?)*

"See, Joe, this guy was really turned off. After Vatican II, his order, like a lot of others, started the updating process. You know, first it was dressing casually around the house . . . then pretty soon, no habit at all. Prayers in community became optional — till soon, no community prayers. For this guy it meant no prayers at all because his whole day was taken up with university activities and all that. Finally, the final stage . . . no faith." *(Why do I have to sit and listen to all this? Why can't he just tell me about himself?)*

"Well, get this, Joe. This guy just picked up and left the priesthood in '68 and really enjoyed the new freedom. Got more involved in research work, but with all this freedom for his research, came the freedom from Christian moral hang-ups too . . . freedom to grow. Know what I mean?"

Joe nodded. *(So what? . . . Get with it!)*

"Here comes the clincher. One day this guy was invited by a bunch of Jesus freaks to join them at a prayer meeting. Well, he kind of laughed at them and told him he had been over that 'religion route' and it didn't have any answers for him. See, these guys knew he was a scientist, so they hit him with, 'Do you give up experimenting if the first experiment is a failure?' So he ended up agreeing to sit in with them. And listen to this, these guys *prayed over him!* No kidding, they all got together and prayed over him. Well, this guy said that while these guys were praying, he really experienced Christ through the Holy Spirit and *bingo!* It brought him back with a vengeance, and now he—"

Joe could wait no longer and interrupted impatiently: "Terrific. So this guy's back . . . but where are you? I haven't been waiting around for a week to hear about some guy I don't even know. For God's sake, will you get to the point?" Joe demanded.

"The *point*, my impatient friend, is that I'm just like this guy. I've had the same experience . . . and *wow!* Praise the Lord!" *(He sounds like a "holy roller" . . . I've never seen Ed act like this before . . . or even get as excited over anything like this before.)*

"Joe, I've found Christ . . . really found Him. I really know Him now!"

"What do you mean, you've 'found Christ'? Who were you preaching before this retreat? Whose sacraments were you administering? Whose sacrifice were you offering? And Who did you learn about all those years in the seminary?"

144

"Okay . . . I know what you're getting at . . . but try to understand. I knew *about* Him, and about His teachings too. Sure, I offered His Holy Sacrifice in the Mass . . . and administered His sacraments, but I *didn't know Him!* I only knew *about* Him! Now He's real! He's alive! Praise Him!" *(I don't believe it! I always knew Ed was an emotional Italian, but I've never seen him like this . . . he's different.)*

"Could I just ask you something? What do you call this experience of yours that has suddenly, after all these years of study and dedicated service, made Christ real? Because to tell you the truth, Ed, I don't know how you or any other priest can manage this life with all its doubts and frustrations if Christ was never truly real."

"This is different, Joe. All of us guys know that it is Christ that keeps us going, that it's Him we are serving. But this 'experience' you asked about is called baptism in the Holy Spirit . . . and it's very Biblical. It suddenly lets Christ completely take over; it makes you more aware; it envelopes you; it lifts—"

"I suppose you speak in tongues now too?" Joe asked with a little "tongue in cheek."

"Go ahead, Joe. You can put me on about it all you want. It doesn't bother me. My Christ is so real, so much a part of me, so strong, that nothing you or anybody else can say, can take that away." Ed's eyes reflected an inner peace that Joe had never seen before, and he felt embarrassed that he had made fun of his friend.

"I'm sorry, Ed, but I'm confused. Along with this new discovery of yours, did you reject the institutional Church? Do you still want to be a priest?"

"Haven't you heard a word I said? I have found Christ and now my priesthood has real meaning. I realize that all my problems were not simply because the pastor and I didn't see eye to eye . . . or because I felt frustrated when I couldn't see the results of my efforts . . . or I was kidding myself into an 'identity crisis' . . . and well, now the crisis is over. I've found myself . . . but I've found myself in Christ. Now I can see the divine nature of the priesthood. Before, I was hung up with only the human nature of it. Can you understand me any better now?"

"I guess," Joe answered, still confused. "But then what were you doing at the chancery?"

"To volunteer for the missions . . . and Christ showed me today that I made the right decision. This was a real experience today!" Ed was smiling. *(God, no . . . not* another *experience, and now the missions?)*

Ed studied the look of disbelief on his friend's face. "Don't you see, Joe? Christ really does speak to us. Before I left the retreat house I felt that it is what He was telling me to do. Now I'm certain. Praise the Lord!"

CHAPTER 9

THE LAST SUPPER

(Friday evening)

(Wonder who left these lights on in the sacristy . . . don't they know that electricity costs money? And look at the missalettes scattered at the end of the pews, it would only take a minute to put them in a neat pile. That carpeting around the altar could do with a good cleaning. Maybe a few of the ladies will volunteer for the job. Must mention it at the next Ladies' Guild . . . which reminds me about the complaints of torn nylons from the vinyl liners on the kneelers — perhaps just a strong tape could take care of that until I can afford to check into it further. Bet that's a costly project. I wish the budget would allow for mosaics behind that large crucifix . . . it would really set it off. Funny, never thought of these things before, but then I was never "the pastor" before . . .)

Joe sat alone in the empty church in the front pew and continued to gaze around as if he were seeing St. Monica's for the first time. He looked at the statue of St. Monica at the side altar and smiled to himself. *(I'm your new pastor!)* But along with the thought came the sobering reality of the responsibility that went along with the new title, sobering enough to bring him to his knees and provoke him to turn his gaze to the large crucifix. *(You know, Lord, it still hasn't sunk in yet. You know also that I'm not really as sure of myself as I made out in the bishop's office this afternoon. Help me to do this job justice, Lord.)*

Joe headed for the sacristy to switch off the lights when the huge clock caught his eye . . . seven o'clock! *(Here I am late again . . . and everybody will be waiting for me. We were supposed to be at Angelo's by now. I can hear Pieri over at the rectory now . . . bet he's blowing a fuse. This is definitely going to be my first project as pastor . . . punctuality!)*

Joe hurried down the middle aisle of the church. After he locked the huge doors he began to run across the parking lot when a voice called out, "Catch, Father Joe!" as a basketball came sailing towards him. Joe caught the ball, dribbled it a few paces then tossed it back to the four eighth-grade boys. "Got time for a few baskets, Father?" one called out.

" 'Fraid not, but catch me next week some night after school, fellas."

Joe hurried through the kitchen and into the den where Ed was seated alone. "Hey, I'm sorry I didn't realize how late it was," Joe explained breathlessly. "Where is everybody?"

"George, Pat and John went in my car . . . George drove. I told them I'd wait around for you so you wouldn't have to drive over alone."

"Want me to turn on the T.V.? . . . or there's some magazines in the rack . . ."

"I'm fine," Ed answered calmly, then reopened the New Testament to the page he held with his index finger and smiled peacefully as he continued to read. *(This is too much! In all the years I've known him this is the first time he didn't lay me out for being late . . . and reads the Bible while he's waiting for me??? Maybe there's something to this "charismatic movement" as he calls it . . . he's sure different . . .)*

It was 7:20 by the time they pulled away from the rectory to keep an appointment that was to start at seven. "How do you get to Angelo's?" Joe asked.

"You're kidding! Angelo is Vince Polesi's father . . . that guy has brought every priest in the diocese there."

"Maybe every priest that was Italian," Joe teased. "That's probably how he got the plush job as head of the radio and T.V. apostolate, wining and dining the hierarchy. Look at Polesi's uncle, Monsignor Rossi — he's the vicar-general. Italians are known for that sort of thing. Just look at all the popes. Did you ever hear of a one called O'Meara, Sullivan, Schneider, or Polaski getting the job?"

Ed just looked at him and grinned. *(How come he's not kidding back? He always has something to come back with when I poke at the Italians. I think I liked him better the other way . . . he's so serious.)*

"Rossi will be there tonight, you know," Ed informed.

"That figures. How did he take it when you asked him about the missions this afternoon?"

"Great, it was the answer to my prayer."

Joe tried to become equally as serious. "Then you're really sure this is what you want? I'm sorry, but I just can't see you being a —"

"Joe, I've never been more sure of anything in my life." Ed's face lit up as he began to illustrate his enthusiasm with his hands. "When I first walked out of Rossi's office, I'll admit that for a few seconds I got cold feet; but when I arrived at your place this afternoon and there was Quinlan telling me about being here to recruit guys from this diocese to go back with him, I knew the Holy Spirit was telling me that I had done the right thing . . . that this is what God really wants me to do. Joe, I prayed for a positive sign and I got it. There's no doubt . . . I'm going!"

Joe shook his head in disbelief. "Well, I hope you can 'speak in tongues' . . . you're going to need it in Bolivia!"

Father Vince Polesi met Joe and Ed at the entrance of the restaurant. "Come on, everybody's here."

Ed shouted something to Father Polesi's father from across the room and he came scurrying over. He went into a long narrative in Italian, swinging his arms and smiling from ear to ear.

"Hold on. Talk English . . . my friend's not Italian," Ed laughed.

"No?" Angelo questioned as he peered at Joe's dark hair.

"No," Joe emphasized, feeling much like an outsider.

"I just tell Father Pieri. Me and Rosa, we say, 'What we gonna do for Vincenzo's good friend, Johnny? He's a been gone so

149

long.' Then we say we fix up a welcome home party he won't forget. So Rosa, she cooks all the food herself and me, I get my best wine. We tell Vincenzo, 'You bring your priest friends to Angelo's and we show them a good time!' "

Mrs. Polesi joined the foursome and extended her hand to Joe. "My husband takes great pleasure in entertaining the clergy, Father. Welcome." She had a small facial resemblance to Monsignor Rossi and it was easy to detect that she, unlike her husband, was American-born.

Angelo, Ed and Father Polesi walked slightly ahead as they went to the private dining room while Mrs. Polesi continued her conversation with Joe laughingly. "Angelo really did it up big tonight. He's always been fond of Father Quinlan ever since he and Vince were friends way back in their high-school days in the seminary. John's been like one of the family; so as soon as Vince phoned and said he arrived, Angelo's been going nonstop preparing for this little get-together tonight. It's so good to see John again."

Joe nodded in appreciation of Mrs. Polesi's sentiment as he followed behind Ed, suddenly realizing that when he left for Bolivia, it will be the first time the two will ever have been really separated bv any meaningful distance since the first day they had entered grade school.

The dining room was elegant; there was one long table set for thirteen at one end of the room, and a temporary bar set up at the other end. Draped in front of the bar was a red banner. In bold yellow print it read: "Welcome Home, Father John." The lights were subdued to almost candlelight effect. Joe saw only a few familiar faces in the room as Father Polesi led them away to introduce them to the other guests who had already broken into small groups.

"This is Father Tom Donlan, the editor of our diocesan paper. And Father Don Walsh, an author . . . and a Dominican. I'm certain if you ask him he'll tell you all about his new book, *Identity Crisis in Religious,*" Father Polesi teased. Joe and Ed shook hands with the pair, then left them to return to their avid conversation about the financial dilemma of Catholic publishers.

"And I think you know this young man," Polesi motioned to Pat, then introduced a Jesuit theologian, Father Carl Hess.

"I was just telling your young friend here, about the danger of nuns placing all their security in a religious habit. I maintain that dress is not what projects the Christ-life within us . . . it's what we are, what we live, what we project through our example as Christians," the theologian stated profoundly. "I work with the Sisters of the Cenacle quite closely and they have combined the necessary functions of all religious — work and prayer in community — and they do it successfully, most of them without a traditional habit."

"Yes," Pat argued, "but a collar or habit does call to mind the presence of Christ. It may be an external, but at a mere glance it reminds the world that here is someone who has chosen to continue Christ's work and I am sure those same Cenacle Sisters could achieve the same success with a habit, right?"

The two went back to their heated dialogue as Polesi led Joe and Ed to the next group. "That's a switch. I thought all the new guys coming up were all for shedding the traditional ways."

"That's because he discovered the Good Shepherd Sisters this afternoon and he was very impressed," Joe explained.

"Here's a man whose work is similar to theirs . . . only he has boys. Father Paul, meet Father Joe Newman and Father Ed Pieri. Father Paul's a Franciscan. And this is Father Ronald Jennings, a retreat master. . . . And of course, you know the guest of honor." The men shook hands and began making small talk. Joe was quite impressed with the spirituality of the Franciscan as he spoke of his work, but suddenly it dawned on him that he had not seen George. He glanced around the room and there isolated from the rest of the guests were George and Monsignor Rossi.

From the look of it, George was doing all the listening, although his eyes never left the floor while Rossi continued to rattle on with his palms outstretched as if he were trying to prove his argument. Joe excused himself and headed toward the pair.

"Congratulations are in order, Joe," Monsignor Rossi offered as he saw Joe approach him. Joe thanked him and began the conversation when George interrupted with, "Anybody want

151

a drink?" and made his way to the bar. It was obvious that he had seized the first opportunity to get away. Rossi inquired about Joe's reaction to his new appointment, but Joe could tell Rossi wasn't interested in his answer as he watched the monsignor's eyes follow George.

Before long Angelo reentered the room and began talking with his brother-in-law.

"Excuse me, Monsignor," Joe murmured as he caught his host's eye.

"Angelo, I think I'll have that drink now," Joe said as he walked away towards George who was slumped over the bar, resting on his elbows as he stared into his refilled glass.

"Nice room, isn't it?" Joe asked in an effort to start the conversation. "Very elegant decor."

"It's nice."

"Bet those cups cost a few bucks," Joe nudged, then motioned towards the dining table where beside each setting lay a gold wine goblet. George turned and the two watched a few waiters enter. Two were carrying wine buckets and one began to place several baskets of French bread on the table.

"Looks like the 'Last Supper,'" Joe joked. "Thirteen places . . . bread and wine."

There was no response from George; instead he lifted his glass and took a very generous drink. Joe persisted. "I'll tell you one thing, the Apostles couldn't have represented such a large cross-section of personalities as the guys we have here tonight. There's a theologian, an author, a retreat master —"

"Yeah," George said indifferently, then turned to face the bar and asked the waiter for another drink as he polished off the rest of his.

Angelo stood before the dining table and began to clap his hands to get the attention of his guests. "Now everybody! You sit down . . . everything is ready. You come and eat."

The groups broke up and began to take their places. Joe and George were the last ones to come to the table, so they took the only two vacant chairs left at the end of the table. There was a single empty place left in the center. Vince Polesi explained that another classmate of his and John's had to cancel at the last minute as one of the waiters carefully removed the place setting.

Monsignor Rossi said grace, then petitioned God to share this meal with His fellow priests. The twelve men made the sign of the cross simultaneously, then took their seats.

"My very best wine!" Angelo boasted, giving the cue to the waiters to begin pouring.

"Is this all we get, Pop — 'bread and wine'?" Vince teased as he held up the empty dinner plate and salad bowl.

Someone at the opposite end of the table picked up on the symbolism of the bread and wine and the twelve places at the table as all the men began to joke good-naturedly about the comparison Joe had voiced to George earlier. George remained silent throughout the salad course while Joe became involved in a lively discussion with the rest of the men concerning the various apostolates the priesthood had to offer.

"Angelo, one thing is certain. Andrew, Matthew, James or John and the rest of the guys didn't eat this well!" John Quinlan complimented as the waiters brought out trays of cannelloni.

"What happened? Did you forget the rest of their names?" Rossi mockingly scolded, then added, "Don't forget Peter. He was probably bossing the whole dinner."

"And Thomas probably went around tasting everything to make sure it was okay," another chimed in.

"And Judas was probably — " Pat halted in the middle of his contribution as he realized he was about to make a very bad joke. Monsignor Rossi, sensing Pat's embarrassment, hastened to sway the group's attention to the sautéing trays the waiters had just placed alongside the main table on which the very best filet mignons had been carefully placed.

George leaned towards Joe. "There's something I have to do . . . be right back." Within five minutes, he returned and slipped back in his chair inconspicuously.

Throughout the rest of the meal, all the priests enjoyed themselves in a lively dialogue. Joe couldn't help but notice that George was paying particular attention to his watch, and that the waiter had already refilled his wine goblet twice. Joe turned away from the rest of the group and tried again to lead George into conversation.

"How's your classes going?"

"Okay."

"Steak's good, isn't it? Just the way I like it . . . medium rare."

"Mine's good, too."

"Was the cannelloni too rich for you?" Joe pointed to George's half-filled side plate with his fork.

"Not very hungry."

"Pat's coming to us is really going to help out with the Sunday Masses, right?"

"Yeah."

"That kid's really filled with zeal, isn't he?"

"Seems to be."

"Of course, I guess all of us come out kind of starry-eyed and ready to convert the whole world . . . don't you think?"

George placed his napkin on the table and moved uncomfortably in his chair, then looked at his watch again. "Joe, I'm going to take off."

Joe quit eating and looked up in surprise. "Why? It's only ten and we're supposed to hang around for a while."

"I know, but I already made plans for later tonight."

"But didn't you drive Ed's car over?"

George reached in his pocket and placed Ed's car keys on the table. "Someone's picking me up here . . . and is probably waiting for me out there now. Make my apologies, will you?" Joe watched him hurry out of the room.

The rest of the evening dragged for Joe as he attempted to join in the celebration. He was relieved when the party began to break up around midnight. Ed permitted Patrick to drive John Quinlan back in his car so he could ride with Joe.

"You don't happen to have a cot or something at your place, do you, Joe? I'm not expected back at Ascension till tomorrow and I hate to wake my mother and father at this hour. They don't know I'm back yet. Thought I'd wait until tomorrow to break the news to them about Bolivia."

"We have plenty of room," Joe explained as the two started for his car. "I'm glad you're riding home with me tonight . . . I'm happy for the company, even if it is 'yours.' "

"Figured you would be . . . you seemed uptight back there. Maybe you'll appreciate me when I'm gone," Ed teased.

"Did George mention anything to you or the others about his plans for later in the evening?" Joe questioned as he slid behind the wheel.

"Not that I remember." Pausing, Ed added quizzically, "How come he took off like that?"

"I don't know. I have to sit down and talk to that guy. He's been acting funny . . . withdrawn . . ."

"Maybe he doesn't like his new pastor!" Ed said, laughing at his own joke. *(Now that's more like it . . . Ed's not completely different. My friend, the "missionary." Still can't believe it!)*

It was after 1 a.m. when Pat, John and Ed retired for the night. "Aren't you going to bed too?" Ed asked.

"In a little while. I want to look at the paper and have another smoke." *(That's a feeble excuse.)*

When Joe was alone in the den, he switched on the T.V. Although he had no intentions of getting engrossed in anything, he felt it would keep him company and perhaps pass the time until George came home. He felt a bit silly, playing the mother hen again, but he rationalized. *(It's different now. As the pastor, I have an obligation to my assistants and I know something's up with George. Still . . . the fastest way to put a wedge between him and me would be to create the impression that I'm keeping close tabs on him. Before, he may have thought I was just an interested friend who wanted to help; but now he's liable to interpret it as the spying pastor who wants to know his assistant's every mood. Better just go to bed . . . I'll talk to him in the morning . . .)*

Joe went to the back door to make certain it was locked, switched off the T.V. and lights in the den, then started down the hall to his room. Once in bed, he began to toss and turn. *(Wish I could sleep . . . I'll be tired as hell in the morning . . . there's the wedding Mass at noon. And I must get the bulletin finished by ten so the secretary can run it off the copier . . . and — the bulletin! I don't even know what's going in it this week!)*

Joe jumped out of bed, slipped on his robe and in his bare

feet, tiptoed to the front parlor office where Monsignor Flannagan kept many of his notes. Joe shuffled a few papers until he found one marked, "Bulletin news." *(This can't be all of it . . . he must have left some on the desk in his room.)*

Back in the pastor's room he found a page that read, "For next week's bulletin." Joe picked up a copy of last week's bulletin lying on the side of the desk; it opened with, "Remarks from the pastor," and consisted of a mere two paragraphs. The closing lines were: "Your pastor, Monsignor Flannagan." *(Guess I'll have to write something to go in this space for this week's bulletin. What am I going to say? "Monsignor Flannagan's too ill to return, so I'm your new pastor. Sorry about that!" This is no time for jokes. Think . . . think!)* He looked at Monsignor's message in last Sunday's bulletin, hoping to find inspiration.

Dear Parishioners:

Last week, it was called to my attention by a fellow priest friend of mine, the outstanding number of attendance at St. Monica's for Mass and Holy Communion, not only for the Sunday Masses, but the weekday Masses as well. I couldn't help but take a sense of pride in our parish . . . for if success is to be measured in any way, it must not be according to the collection or the attendance at last week's guild meetings or last season's parish dance, but rather it must be measured by the number who seek to find God in the sacraments administered to them by their parish priests.

We priests at "your" St. Monica's thank you. You have made our ministry here most rewarding by your faithful support and encouragement. That St. Monica's may continue to receive the Good Lord's Choicest Blessings is the wish of us all.

Your pastor,
Monsignor William J. Flannagan

(Did he know this would be the last bulletin he would write?)

Joe looked around the empty room till his eyes rested on the

156

bedstand where there lay a black rosary and a prayer book frayed and faded with age. On the dresser was a huge picture of the face of Christ and two small golf trophies on either side. *(What is it he always said? "I have two loves in my life, God and golf, but always in that order!")* Joe smiled at the simulated shrine as he remembered Flannagan's words. He began paging through the ledger at the side of the desk, then through the bills clipped to a board; memos were scattered here and there. His head began to swim. Joe gathered the necessary papers and headed back to his room and his own desk. The only light in the room was from the small desk lamp. *(All those nights I used to see only a dim crack of light coming from beneath Flannagan's door . . . now I know what he was doing.)*

After placing the messages of each parish organization in sequence, Joe took a blank sheet of paper and a pen and began to write, "Remarks from the pastor . . ." *(From the pastor! What do I say?)* He felt guilty. He had enjoyed the congratulations from his fellow priests this very evening, and wasn't there a particular sense of pride when it was pointed out that he was one of the youngest pastors in the diocese? And wasn't he pleased by his parents' praise at their son's new appointment? *(Now how do I go about it? My first task as pastor, a message in the parish bulletin, and I can't think of one thing to say . . .)* Joe crumpled up the paper, then reached for another clean sheet. He began to write once again, "Remarks from the pastor . . ." *(No, that sounds conceited for a newcomer to the job.)* Joe scratched out the line and wrote, "Message to my parishioners . . ." *("My parishioners!" That sounds pretentious too.)* Joe crumpled the second sheet and threw it in the wastebasket. He rubbed his head as if he were trying to bring all the right thoughts to the surface. *(I can't think.)* He looked at the clock on the bedstand . . . 2 a.m. *(I'll write it in the morning . . . the main news is already laid out. I'm too tired to concentrate.)* Joe turned out the light and stumbled to his bed, pulled the covers over his shoulders, then lay on his side. *(Too sleepy to concentrate and too wound up to sleep!)*

A car pulled up in front of the rectory; Joe recognized George's voice. He leaped out of bed and peered through the slightly cracked slats of the venetian blinds. George got out of the car, slammed the door of the passenger's side, then leaned his head and shoulders through the open window for an unusually long time. *(What's he doing? Who's he talking to?)* George's figure masked the driver. Finally, he stood upright, and walked toward the front door. Joe caught just a brief glimpse of the driver as the car pulled away. *(It's a girl! . . . Hold on . . . I'm jumping to conclusions. I'm doing the same thing I complained about when the person mistook the situation between Gregg and me Sunday night. Still. . . the figure seemed quite small. Forget it, Newman . . . . you're guessing . . . only guessing.)*

Joe returned to his bed and folded his hands behind his head as he lay on his back staring into the darkness. Within minutes he heard George close the door in his room. He waited and listened. *(What's he doing in there?)* He could hear George shuffling about. *(Don't tell me he's hanging up his clothes, for a change.)* Joe remembered the clutter in George's room that morning he had gone in there to retrieve his cassock. Joe turned to his other side. *(Why can't I sleep? Wasting all these precious minutes of sleep. As long as I'm just lying here, maybe I should try to write something . . .)* Joe got out of bed for the third time, grabbed a few clean sheets of paper and a magazine to use as a writing board. He turned on the bedside light, lay on his stomach and began: "Dear parishioners . . ." *(That sounds better.)* "Today, I have bad news for you . . ." *(I can't say "bad news." Then they'll think I don't want to be their pastor. I never could write . . .)* Joe remembered how he labored through his composition assignments during all his years of schooling. Now, a fully mature man, he found the task no more palatable. Joe rested his head on his arms, said a prayer to the Holy Spirit to help him find the right words, then began to write once again.

Dear Parishioners:

I am asking today that you remember in your prayers, our devoted pastor, Monsignor Flannagan, who is quite ill. If you'll recall his remarks to you in last week's bulletin, he stated that a parish's success could not be measured by its size or contributions, but rather "by the number who seek to find God in the sacraments administered to them by their parish priests." But surely the number of attendance would not have been as great if it were not for the patient leadership of Monsignor Flannagan. It was he who worked so hard to provide your children with a school where they could develop not only in the arts and sciences, but in a sound religious training. It was he who fought to bring to that school the finest caliber of religious to teach your children. It was he who started the various organizations, the Ladies' Guild, the Teen Club, the Men's Club, the Athletic Club, the Men and Women's choir, the Teen Choir, and the Altar Society. And it was he who worked so tirelessly at all the fundraising projects to build for you a magnificent place of worship, St. Monica's Church. The measure of his success as pastor cannot be judged by the number of stone structures or the increase of parish members within St. Monica's boundaries, but rather in the fond regards of his parishioners.

As your new pastor, I need your support and prayers to keep the spirit of St. Monica's. Together we will make it a lasting tribute to a great pastor and a dear friend, Monsignor Flannagan.

Yours in Christ,
Father Joseph Newman

Joe placed the writing material on the bedstand and turned out the lights, hopefully for the last time. It was already 3 a.m. He grasped the pillow around his head as if to shut out all his anxieties and surrender to the sleep he needed so desperately. (*Lord, You know all my weaknesses. Knowing them, why did You want to make me a pastor? When I think of all the bills, running the parish school, keeping the nuns happy, the lay staff happy, the parishioners happy, running all those organizations, and working in harmony with two men completely different than myself, Benetti and George — especially George! — filling Flannagan's shoes isn't going to be an easy job. Lord, I hope You know what You're doing. Flannagan's shoes never looked so big . . .*)

CHAPTER 10

COMMITMENT

(Saturday)

Joe was awakened at 6:45 by the pounding on a nearby door and Dearie's voice calling, "Father George! Father George! Are you awake?"

Joe crawled out of bed, grabbed his robe and headed for the hallway.

"What's going on?"

"Father Joe, it's almost time for the seven o'clock Mass and I don't think Father Rahner is up yet . . ."

"George!" Joe called. When there was no response, he opened the door to the unoccupied room. There was an envelope on the neatly made bed; it was addressed to Joe. Still not completely awake, he sat on the bed and rubbed his eyes. Tearing open the envelope, he began to read its contents.

Dear Joe:

I guess you'll think I took the coward's way out by not telling you face to face that I'm leaving, but I know you'll hit me with a thousand reasons why I should consider staying and I've thought of all of them myself. Nothing can persuade me to stay now. It's not a spur-of-the-moment thing with me. I've been knocking it around for some time, but tonight at the dinner, I knew I didn't fit in. I guess I've always known it. Anyway, this is kind of a lousy trick to play on you your first day, but I know

there's enough guys in the house to help you out over the weekend and I just can't cut it one more day.

You've been good to work with, so good luck with your
new job. I know you'll hear it sooner or later, so I'll tell you
myself: Wish me luck; I'm getting married.

Peace,
George

"My God!" Joe said, looking at the paper in disbelief.

"What's all the commotion about out here?" Ed yawned as
he stood in the doorway.

Ed's voice brought Joe back from his shocked stupor. "Ed,
take the seven for me right away, will you? I'll explain later."

Within fifteen minutes, Joe entered the kitchen — show-
ered, shaved and fully dressed. Dearie was seated at the table
wringing her hands.

"It was bad news, wasn't it, Father Joe?"

Joe explained the contents of George's letter, knowing that
Dearie respected all confidences exchanged within the rectory
walls. "Wake John, will you, and ask him to take the eight
o'clock Mass . . . and the bulletin news is on my bedstand, in case
I'm not back in time to give it to the secretary. I'm going to find
George. He may tell me to mind my own damn business, but I
must try."

Joe ran his index finger down the "R's" in the telephone directory, RAH, RAHN . . . RAHNER, Alan, Frederick, George.
(I'll try this one . . . maybe he's a junior.) Joe dialed the number.
*(How can I ask for George without worrying them? Still, if he's
there, they'll tell me right away.)*

"Hello?" came the voice from the other end.

"Mrs. Rahner?"

"Yes, who's calling, please:"

"Is George there? *Father* George?"

"No, who's calling?" *(Now what should I tell her?)*

Hello? Is someone there?" she asked again.

"Mrs. Rahner, this is Father Newman. I was wondering if

161

George may have stopped by this morning on his way for an appointment. I wanted to tell him something." *(This sounds dumb. Who is going to keep an appointment this hour in the morning?)*

"Oh, Father Newman . . ." she said slowly, as if trying to place the name. "No, George hasn't stopped by here, but he usually stops by on Saturdays. Shall I have him call you?"

Joe hesitated. "Uh . . . please . . . if you will."

"Father, is there something wrong? I get the feeling . . ." Now she hesitated. "Something is wrong, isn't it? Didn't George come home last night?" *(How does she know?!!)*

"He came home but he left before I could talk to him this morning."

"You mean he didn't say Mass?"

"Well, as a matter of fact . . . no, he didn't."

"I was afraid something like this was going to happen. Father, do you suppose you could come over?" Her voice was worried.

"I'll be right there."

George's father answered the door of the Rahner home and invited Joe to the kitchen where his wife had already set places for coffee. "Sit down, Father, we can talk here. The girls are still sleeping . . . I don't want thém in on this." The two teen-age girls in the family portrait flashed in Joe's mind as he nodded in agreement.

"Father, this is a little embarrassing for us. Did George give you any idea where he was going?" Mrs. Rahner asked.

"Not really, he just said he was leaving . . . didn't say where."

"Leaving the priesthood, I take it. I'm not surprised. I saw it coming," Mr. Rahner said disgustedly. "I'll bet it's that girl, Marge Harris. He's run off with her."

"Then you know the girl involved?"

Mrs. Rahner sat down and poured the coffee. In a very anxious voice she began: "George brought her here several times. Mind you, we've never condoned this from the start. It seemed quite innocent at first though. She's a social worker and attends many of the meetings in the inner-city projects. She and George were on the same committees. Soon, he was picking her up and taking her home from these meetings because he said it was too rough a neighborhood for her to drive down alone. That sounded reasonable. In fact, that's the first time we met her, on their way to one of those meetings last spring. Well, George began to talk about her almost all the time and I got the feeling they were seeing each other quite often. Finally, just about two months ago, my husband and I could stand it no longer so we told George how we felt . . . that a priest had no business keeping company with a lady friend. He kept insisting it wasn't what we imagined; but you know, Father, we've lived longer and we felt George was putting blinders on, that he was becoming more and more involved with this young woman. Apparently, he told her how we felt because she called here one afternoon and asked to talk with me. She told me that I shouldn't worry, that she and George were mature adults and that their relationship was simply a deep friendship. She even came over one day to visit with me. You know, I couldn't help but like the girl. She seemed so sincere, but — "

"But George is a priest!" the father interrupted.

"You don't happen to have her address, do you?" Joe asked.

"I'll get it." Mrs. Rahner left the table.

"I don't like it, Father . . . don't like it one bit," Mr. Rahner stated in his deep voice. "If George wants to make trouble for himself, I have no sympathy for him."

"Here it is," Mrs. Rahner said as she returned, handing the slip of paper to Joe and adding, "Are you going there now?"

"Yes, I'll get in touch with you later."

"Make him change his mind, Father, please," Mrs. Rahner pleaded, her eyes brimming with tears. "George is a priest, and I — " She covered her mouth with her handkerchief as she broke down and began to cry.

Miss Harris' plush apartment was just a fifteen-minute drive away. Joe went directly to the room number specified after the address. A girl in her late twenties, dressed in a chic beige suit, answered. She said nothing for a few seconds after she noticed Joe's collar, then finally she called out, "George! I think

163

there's someone here for you." *(That's the girl in the photo . . . the one with George in the boat!)*

"For me?" George, dressed in a dark olive suit and tie, walked to the doorway, "Joe!" he exclaimed in astonishment.

"Got a minute, George?" Surprisingly, Joe's voice was steady, not betraying one trace of nervousness.

"Come in," George managed and pointed to the living room directly leading from the foyer where four bags were packed.

Joe took the single chair across from the couch while Marge Harris and George simultaneously sat on the couch taking each other's hand as if to offer mutual support.

"I take it you got my note. But how did you find me here?" George asked, furrowing his brow. "Oh, you talked to my parents," he added reluctantly.

"Apparently they had some idea this was about to happen," Joe offered.

"I hope you didn't come here to talk me out of it, Joe."

"I just wanted to try and make you reconsider . . . to give yourself a little time. You don't trade a collar for a wedding band in the same day and still remain sure of yourself."

"Joe, I have thought about it. You asked me the other night about my visit with Rossi. I didn't say anything to you then, but we didn't talk just about that demonstration in front of the chancery and the T.V. interview. He asked me if I was content in the priesthood and I gave him an honest answer: *No!* I made up my mind then that I'd give myself one more month to try and work things out: but last night at that party for John, and being with all those priests, I knew I didn't fit in. I was uncomfortable. I wasn't one of them . . . I don't think I ever was."

"But jumping right into a marriage — are you prepared for this, both of you?" Joe fixed his eyes on Marge.

"I am, Father . . . and I think George is too. I know him and I believe I know how to make him happy. There are obstacles but we can overcome them." Marge tightened her grip on George's hand.

"We love each other, Joe," George said. "We could be dishonest and I could continue living a facade, but that's not the right way."

"Then there's nothing I can say?" Joe felt defeated.

"You could wish us luck," George half-smiled.

"What about your parents?"

"I'll call them and explain things before we leave. And listen, if it's okay, I'll send one of my brothers over to pick up the rest of my things."

Joe nodded, then reluctantly stood to leave. Never before had he felt so much like an intruder.

George took his hand when they reached the doorway. "Good luck as pastor. You'll do a good job. I told you the other night, you're cut out for the priesthood — no hang-ups. Remember?"

Joe looked closely at him, then said simply, "Take care," and walked away.

Joe slowly climbed into his car and was about to pull away from the curb when a voice stopped him. "Father Newman, wait up!"

Marge Harris opened the door on the passenger's side. "Father, I wanted to talk to you just a second. Please don't judge George and me. It just happened . . . we fell in love. I'm Catholic, Father, and I know what we're bucking but understand, if you can, we love each other. Perhaps you can't realize what that means; but it means that George is the most important thing in my life . . . he's a part of me. I want to take care of him, have his children, make him happy . . . do for him what every woman wants to do for the man she loves. The fact that he is a priest doesn't change this. There is just one other thing. The last thing I want for George is for him to be made to feel as an outcast because of his love for me . . . so, Father, could you keep in touch? It would mean so much to George . . . and also to me. Try not to judge us, Father. Please try to understand." There were tears in her eyes.

"Tell George if he needs someone to talk to, he knows where to find me . . . that goes for you too. In the meantime, I'll pray for both of you." That was all Joe could offer as she left the car. *("The fact that he is a priest . . ." But that's just the point: he has no right to give his love, or accept hers. "It just happened . . . we fell in love . . ." Does this collar I'm wearing harness every natu-*

165

ral emotion in a man? Is it possible that I too could fall in love? Could it "just happen" to me? "Perhaps you can't realize what it means . . . ." Maybe she's right . . . maybe I can't . . .)

Mercy Hospital was just minutes away from the apartment house and since it was still not quite ten, he decided to pay a quick call to Monsignor Flannagan.

"And how is the new pastor of St. Monica's? Congratulations!" Flannagan tried to affect a cheerful manner, but his features and color betrayed his discomfort and pain. "Roll me up a bit, will you, Joe?" He motioned to the lever at the end of the bed. Joe continued to turn until Flannagan was almost to an upright position. "That's good. Now sit down and fill me in on the news." *(Some news . . . twenty-four hours as pastor and I've already lost an assistant.)*

"I'm afraid it's not too good."

"Nothing can be as bad as all that . . . suppose you just tell me."

"It's George . . . he left this morning."

"I see . . ." The sick man's expression changed.

"I just left him now. When I got his note this morning, I decided to go after him . . . I guess it was stupid, but I felt like at least I had to try to talk to him. I flunked out." Joe unconsciously began to pound the palm of his hand with his fist. "I fell flat on my face."

Flannagan studied Joe for a minute, realizing some of his frustration. "Don't be so hard on yourself, Joseph. Let me give you just a word of advice from an old man who has put in a lot of years in the job you were just hired for. When I first became the pastor of St. Monica's, there was an old retired priest in residence there . . . he was a very wise man. One day he sat me down and gave me something to hang on to all these years . . . now I'm passing it on to you. Don't blame yourself for everything that goes wrong — and don't take the credit for everything that goes right. Remember it well . . . it comes in handy."

Joe relaxed a little. "I just felt so useless . . . there was really nothing I could say," he explained.

"I'm certain of that. I've been picking up discontented vibrations from George for a while now . . . in fact, I think I even inferred that to you a few days ago, if I recall. No, Joe, I feel this was almost inevitable . . . just a shame it had to happen your first day, huh?"

"I'll survive," Joe grinned, attempting to change the mood. "And how are you feeling?"

"I'm in no shape for golf," Flannagan joked, "but those shots they're giving me kind of takes the edge off things."

A nurse entered. "Monsignor, what are you doing sitting up all the way like that?" she scolded, then turned the lever to bring him back down to keep his chest and head just slightly above his hips. She reinserted the I.V. tube into his left arm. "Are you comfortable?"

"For the time being."

She fluffed the pillows behind his head and tucked the hospital covers snugly at the bottom sides of the bed. "There now," she said, satisfied with her efforts. "Just ring if you need anything."

Flannagan waited until she left the room. "I hate all this fussing about . . . takes away a man's dignity."

Joe spent the next half hour filling the monsignor in on the happenings of the past week and Flannagan informed him of a few pending projects. Finally when it was almost eleven, Joe rose to leave. "I have the Stanton wedding at twelve. Do you need anything before I go?"

"Yes, do you have time to hear my confession?" *(He wants me to hear his confession? I know Rossi and Bishop Condry have been here to visit . . . why is he asking me?)*

Joe sat down again, reached into his breast pocket and placed the stole around his neck; he bent slightly forward on the bed, shielding his eyes with his hands.

"Bless me, Father, for I have sinned . . ." the older priest began. "This is a general confession, Joe."

Within ten minutes, the pastor had revealed all the weaknesses of his sixty-five years. He closed his eyes. With his hands folded on his chest, he said devoutly, "For these and all the sins of my past life, I am heartily sorry."

Joe raised his hand for absolution. "I absolve you from your

167

sins, in the name of the Father, and of the Son, and of the Holy Spirit . . ."

"Thanks, Joe." Flannagan took his hand.

"Thank you, Monsignor." Joe was humbled by the old man's request and subsequent appreciation. He watched Flannagan take a deep breath, then turn his gaze towards the window.

"Clear day . . . good day for golf, or a wedding. Now run along . . ."

Joe hurried from the room. Flannagan was too proud a man to accept the pity that Joe was certain showed in his own expression. *(God, I'm crying! I've been living with that man for the past three years and never once did I realize just how good a man he was . . . or how much his friendship means to me . . .)*

Joe was about to step on the elevator when he spied Nowaski coming down the corridor. Joe blew his nose quickly. "Good morning, Doctor."

"Got a cold?"

"Just sinus . . . all stopped up." The doctor gave him a rather skeptical look.

"Did you see Bill already?"

"Yes . . . how is he? I mean 'really'?"

Nowaski gave no answer: he just shook his head negatively, saying, "But he's got guts . . . that old thickhead's really got guts." Then he walked to his friend's room wearily.

Joe went directly to the sacristy to vest as time was running short and he wasn't about to be late for his first Mass as pastor, much less a nuptial Mass. "Good crowd for the we▒▒▒▒," Joe said as he peeked out at the assembled congregation.

"Hey, Father, think this Mass will be over by one?" asked the altar boy as he straightened his surplice. "I got a soccer game, and it's a big one too."

"I'll work on it, Mark," Joe laughed as he tousled the boy's red hair. *(Kid, you're lucky . . . your biggest worry is whether you'll be late for a soccer game.)*

Joe watched the bride's expression as he waited for the couple to approach the altar. Rosemary was beautiful: she was smiling as if she could not contain her joy. Joe thought of another bride he had seen today. She had tears too, but not like Rosemary's ... Marge Harris' tears were sad. Joe said a prayer for her and George and begged God to help them through what looked to be a hard road ahead. She had said herself, "There are many obstacles ..."

When it came time in the ceremony to exchange their vows, Joe thought of George again. He had taken the same vows as Joe, different from the ones he would take today. Could Marge ever feel certain that those vows would be kept? ... or broken as the ones that he made at his ordination? Joe tried to keep his attention on the bride and groom before him. Frank was lucky: he was sure of himself. He had tried the religious life, but God redirected him before he had made the perpetual binding pledge ... if only that same thing could have happened in George's case. Rosemary and Frank, unlike Marge and George, could come to each other today, certain that God was a part of their union. Perhaps one day priests will be able to do the same ... but until then, it is meant to be a sacrifice.

"Just in time for lunch, Father Joe," Dearie greeted at the door, then in a lower voice added, "Did you talk to Father George?"

"Talked to him, but didn't get anywhere." Joe took his place at one end of the table; John and Pat were at either side. "Where's Father Benetti?"

"In his room listening to his music ... he said he didn't want any lunch. He hasn't left his room since breakfast when he heard the news."

"I'll talk to him when I'm through."

"You look beat," John Quinlan said sympathetically. "Why don't you let me take the afternoon confessions for you? I don't have any plans this afternoon and Mom and I have been catching up on all the gabbing this morning."

"Thanks ... I'll catch a few winks before it's time. I could use your help at the evening session, though. We usually have more come for confession then."

"Fine."

"Father Joe, I took a call for you this morning, a Mrs. Froman . . . or was it Forest . . . no, it was . . ." Dearie stopped as a puzzled look crossed her face.

"Ferris?" Joe prompted.

"That's it! Well she was really put out. Said that she hoped something would be done about all those drinks being served at the Men's Club Tuesday night because — let me see, how did she put it? — oh, yeah . . . 'Because it was unbecoming for Christians to be drinking heavily on Church property!' "

Joe shrugged. "What else is new?"

"Pardon?" Pat asked, confused.

"Pat, if you're going to be here anytime at all, you'll hear from Mrs. Ferris at least three times a week . . . but that's only if things are running smoothly. Mrs. Ferris is a 'professional' Christian."

"In Bolivia," John laughed, "when I get a 'Mrs. Ferris,' I always say, *'No comprendo español muy bien.'* "

Joe hated to dampen the mood, but he had to bring it up. "Since George is gone, John, could you take his Masses tomorrow? I'll contact Rossi to see about a permanent weekend supply Monday."

"Sure, is there anything else? I can take his weekday Masses this coming week."

"Good, then in next week's bulletin, I'll explain that we'll revise the weekday schedule to two Masses — 6:15 and 8:00 . . . at least for the time being unless he can spare another assistant."

"I'll be here for all the Sunday Communions. I can handle the sick calls Friday too," Pat added eagerly.

When Joe approached Benetti's room he could hear the strains of "The Sound of Music." Joe knocked gently.

"Come in," Benetti called out as he lowered the volume. "Beautiful music, Father, beautiful. This is the album Father Rahner gave me." The old man looked melancholy.

Joe pulled the chair away from the desk. "Father Quinlan has offered to help us out this coming week."

Benetti ignored Joe's statement. Instead he began to talk

about something that was obviously bothering him. "You know, Joseph, I was hard on him, but I like him. In his own way, he was kind."

"Father Benetti, surely you don't feel anything you said to George provoked his leaving?"

"No, no, but he must have had much trouble in here." Benetti held his hands to his heart. "I just didn't see it . . . or make it any easier for him either."

"Well, Father, we can't be thinking about all that anymore . . . we have a large parish to run. You and I have to get down to business and keep it going despite the fact that we've lost two priests this week. I'm going to need all the help you can give me," Joe said, trying to break the old man's despondent mood.

Benetti nodded in agreement. "I'll help you with the afternoon confessions."

"Good," Joe replied enthusiastically as he replaced the chair and began to leave.

"Joseph . . ." Benetti reached for several papers on his small desk and held up one of the fresh new bulletins that had just come off the copier. "Your bulletin was very good. St. Monica's will be proud of you." *(And I thought he'd hit me with something like, "I told you so . . .")*

Saturday afternoon confessions began at four o'clock and ended at 5:30, in order to allow enough time to prepare for the Saturday evening folk Mass. Today, it was unusually slow, and several times Joe found himself drifting off as he read a book of meditations between penitents. He spent a great deal of time with an eight-year-old boy who knew he was going to hell because he kicked his cat; the fact that he beat up his little sister wasn't his capitol sin, for, he explained, "My cat never treats me mean, or teases me, or takes my toys, or gets me in trouble!"

At 5:30 on the dot, Joe emerged from the confessional and stepped outside the church for a smoke before vesting for Mass. A few of the teens were already arriving with their guitars. A young man pulled up in his car, found a parking space and came running up the walk to Joe. "Am I late for confession, Father?"

The face looked vaguely familiar. He was a good-looking

young man, neatly dressed with short well-groomed hair. "It's me, Father . . . don't you remember?"

"Gregg?" Joe said questioningly.

"I know what you're going to say. You didn't recognize me with the haircut and clean clothes. That's all I've been hearing since last Tuesday. Anyway, Father, I told you I would be here to see you, so here I am!"

"And you want to go to confession?" Joe was still a little stunned.

"Yeah, I have to keep a promise . . . I promised God if I beat this rap, I'd go back to the sacraments."

"I read about your trial. Congratulations." Joe stamped out his cigarette as Gregg followed him to the confessional.

Once inside, Joe slid the small grille away.

"You're going to have to help me out, Father. It's been a long time."

"Just start talking, Gregg. I'm listening."

Gregg awkwardly recalled his sins, lack of faith, absence from the sacraments, indulgence in sex, drug-taking, stealing, lying, but mostly, his selfishness. "For these and all my sins, I'm really sorry, Father." He uttered the final words as if he were suddenly aware of his shame.

Joe absolved Gregg from his sins, then gave the appropriate penance. When Gregg finished his act of contrition, Joe asked, "Where do you go from here? I know the tension of the trial prompted your return to the sacrament of penance, but now what?"

"I won't lie to you, Father. Being faced with a possible jail sentence kind of makes a believer out of you . . . but I still have hang-ups about this religion thing . . . like going to Mass on Sunday. I just can't believe you can go to hell if you miss. You know, Father, a couple of times when I tried to get back, I'd go to Mass; but hearing about next week's parish carnival or some bingo affair, just turned me off. I got more out of sitting by the river or, listening to folk songs . . . follow me?"

"I know what you mean, but God didn't give the commandment, 'Remember to keep holy down by the river listening to folk songs.' Gregg, why don't you stay for Mass? It's the teen folk

Mass, geared to the young people. Stay ... maybe you'll get *turned on!*"

Pat was already running through a few songs with the folk group when Joe walked down the side aisle on his way to the sacristy. The kids seemed to be hanging on his every word. An idea occurred.

"Pat, after the Gospel reading, the pulpit is all yours."

"What?"

"I said you can take the homily today ... no time like the present to jump right in there and 'do your thing'!"

" 'Do my thing'? I don't even know what to talk about. I'm not prepared. I never gave a sermon before and look at how packed the church is, and ..." Pat stammered.

"Good experience," Joe interrupted, then hurried away to vest for Mass.

Joe was proud of the way Pat handled himself. He gave the congregation, mostly young people, fifteen minutes of the kind of dialogue they could understand. What was more, he coupled his "now" way of talking with sound theology. At the start of the homily, Joe had doubts as to whether he had misplaced his confidence in Pat, but as soon as Pat got through the first two minutes, he took command. It seemed he was so intent on the message he was trying to convey, that every trace of self-consciousness was gone. Instead, there stood a young man committed to his ideals, eloquently sharing them with his audience.

"Neat sermon, Father," a young girl opined as she left the church. "Liked what you had to say," a teen-age boy said as he passed to catch up with his friends. "Really enjoyed the Mass tonight, Father," another praised. Pat continued to accept the compliments as the congregation filed out. He was beaming.

"Can I have your autograph?" Joe teased when they were finally alone.

Pat grinned: he knew he had done well. "They liked it, Father," he said, relieved.

"Must have, I only counted three yawns while you were talking." They both laughed.

CHAPTER 11

HE WHO LAUGHS LAST

(Saturday night)

"I'm not in the mood for a wedding reception, but I promised to be there. Want to go over to the church hall for a while, John?"

"Okay with me . . . soon as I change."

"Good, maybe Pat will want to come too." Joe locked the church doors, then offered John a cigarette. The two men walked across the parking lot slowly, enjoying the evening breeze. Cars were already starting to fill the pavements as the guests arrived.

"Ed called this afternoon. He invited me to visit with his parents tomorrow . . . kind of explain my work in Bolivia. He said they've resigned themselves to his leaving, but they have a thousand questions."

"Good idea," Joe agreed. "What made you volunteer for the missions?" he asked as an afterthought.

"My decision never came as dramatically as Ed's. I was an assistant in a north county parish. Things were going well . . . too well, maybe. I had a very steady diet of a luxurious rectory, affluent parishioners and a minimal amount of work. I felt more like a social director than a priest. My duties were almost becoming mechanical. It was a very small parish, no school and too little demand on the priests. I didn't feel that I was accomplishing anything. I felt my ordination equipped me with more potential than just the social obligation of uttering niceties to the rich. So when a priest visited the parish to ask for financial support for his poor Bolivian parish, I talked with him a bit.

There was an overwhelming need down there . . . the people were starving, both physically and spiritually. I hashed it over for about a year, then finally made the decision and here I am."

"Are you happy?"

"I'll put it this way . . . I'm satisfied that my priesthood is serving so many, but I get frustrated when I see how much there is to do with just a handful of priests and funds to work with. I know one thing, Joe, the priests down there have little time to suffer that prevalent malady you have here: the 'identity crisis' . . . and being 'too busy.' " The two men paused outside the rectory to finish their cigarettes. "I'm fulfilled . . . my work is meaningful. I suppose that's all any priest can ask." John searched his own thoughts. "Yes, Joe, I guess you could say I'm happy."

"But isn't it a hard adjustment, living in a different culture?"

"You become acclimated; but there's one thing I still miss badly . . . pro football," John laughed.

"There's a game next Saturday night, and you're my guest."

"I'll hold you to it."

Joe opened the door, letting John enter first. *(I like him . . . wish Rossi would send me an assistant as solid as John . . .)*

The reception was well under way when Joe, Pat and John arrived at the hall. The band began playing a fox-trot as guests crowded the dance floor. "Lots of parishioners here tonight. You'll get a chance to meet them," Joe said as he recognized several faces coming toward them. Soon he was besieged with questions about Flannagan's condition and his new appointment. John was carted away to a table by a man who recognized him from their high-school days and Pat stood close to Joe's side as he introduced the new parish deacon. After about fifteen minutes, the bride and groom rescued the pair from their interrogators and ushered them to the huge punch bowl equipped with a floating block of ice shaped like a heart.

"There's a bar set up over there, Father. Which do you prefer?" Frank asked.

"The punch is fine." *(If I drink anything stronger, I'm liable to fall asleep right here on my feet.)*

175

"Fine for me too," Pat agreed.

A few newcomers arrived and greeted the bride and groom while the band went into a rock number. "Man, this music kills me . . . can't stand still," Pat whispered as he moved his head in rhythm to the music, but not too conspicuously.

"Well, whatever you do, don't break into the 'bugaloo' because here come Rhona Barett of St. Monica's," Joe said from the side of his mouth, then in a much louder, and professional voice . . . "Good evening, Mrs. Ferris."

"Good evening, Father."

"See ya," Pat whispered as he walked away to mingle. *(He catches on fast.)*

"Congratulations. One man's gain is another man's loss," she said accusingly.

"Unfortunate, but true." *(Biddy!)*

"Did you taste the punch, Father? It's very good. I think it's very considerate of the host to offer the guests an alternative to all that liquor for those of us who do not care to drink."

"Agreed." Joe raised his punch cup to make certain Mrs. Ferris would place him in her preferred category.

"You know my husband . . . Henry."

Henry Ferris, a shy, timid little man, extended his limp hand.

"Mr. Ferris, how are you?" Joe asked cordially.

"Henry's fine," she answered. "We don't usually go to these affairs but since the bride's mother and I have worked on so many committees together, we made an exception." She paused long enough to sip her punch. "Notice all the 'long-hairs' tonight? Father Rahner would feel right at home." She giggled sarcastically. *(Thank God the news about George hasn't leaked out yet. She sure as hell wouldn't be smiling . . . on second thought, maybe she would!)*

The punch bowl was behind Mrs. Ferris and therefore was out of her view. As she continued airing her suggestions about the various parish organizations, Joe watched over her shoulder as two laughing groomsmen, apparently feeling the effects of the celebration, dumped in two fifths of vodka, then quickly stirred the punch around.

". . . And I was telling Henry the other day . . . I don't know why he even goes to the Men's Club. What constructive projects have they come up with in the past three months? It seems to me that they concentrate only on having a good time. If you ask me, I think the half of them see it as an excuse just to get out of the house." She paused again and handed Henry her glass. "Would you like some more too, Father?"

"No, thanks. I'm fine, Mrs. Ferris." In an effort to cover up his amusement about what she was about to taste in her next cup, he said, "And you were saying?"

"Oh, yes . . . well . . ." She sipped her refill. "Mmmm . . . just like Cana. They've saved the 'best for last'!"

Joe could contain himself no longer. "Mrs. Ferris, I hate to end our conversation, but someone over there is trying to get my attention. If you'll excuse me . . ." Joe walked away, not too certain where he was heading, but anyone would be a merciful change from what he had just left.

"Father Newman!" Joe turned to find Mrs. Davis heading towards him. "Father, we would like to have you join our table for a little while. But I came over to talk to you a second in private, before you go over there."

"Surely, but let me tell you first, you have nothing to worry about." Joe was certain she wanted to know more about Pam's frame of mind. "I was at the Good Shepherd Convent yesterday and the nuns assured me that Pam is doing very well and she seems quite content in her new surroundings."

"Yes, I know." She dismissed his pleasant information, then in a very confidential voice, said, "I just wanted to tell you before you came to the table not to mention Pam or that home. We told our friends that she was away at school. I mean . . . I'd just die if any of them knew the truth . . . besides, that is partly true. She is away . . . and it is a school too. You will be discreet, won't you?" she pleaded as she sashayed to the waiting table, smiling broadly. (*Poor Pam . . . it's no wonder . . .*)

Joe made his visit as short as possible at the Davis table, then excused himself again, explaining that he must circulate. (*And besides that, I could use that drink about now . . .*) He walked past the punch bowl where Henry was busy pouring two

177

more drinks. He smiled to himself as he approached the bar.

"Father Joe, how are you? What do you think of that intermediate soccer team of ours? We beat Immaculate Conception today!" informed Mr. Kramer, the head of the Athletic Association.

"Terrific," Joe answered with projected enthusiasm, then ordered a weak bourbon and soda. After ten minutes with Mr. Kramer and a firm promise that he would permit his organization to have a dance to raise money for uniforms, he made his way toward Pat who seemed to be cornered by a woman in her forties. She was ostentatiously dressed and she swayed slightly as she lifted her drink. "I think priests should be able to dance . . . . . after all, they're human. A little fun never hurt anyone and I don't see anything wrong with dancing." She smiled girlishly. "You're a cute one. Where have you been all my life?"

"I wasn't alive for half of it, Ma'am," Pat replied, smiling like an innocent schoolboy, then walked away.

Joe turned away as he began to laugh; he didn't want to add insult to injury.

"Think she'll be mad because I was rude?" Pat questioned a little remorsefully.

"Probably won't even remember it. Besides, I don't recognize her as one of our parishioners, so we're home free."

Joe and Pat spied a couple of empty chairs at the opposite end of the hall. "Let's grab a seat for a few minutes, then we can cut out gracefully," Joe suggested. The pair passed the huge punch bowl again. This time Mrs. Ferris was pouring two more. The band started up again with another rock number as the younger crowd began dancing.

"Look at them, Henry. It's shameful . . . all that twisting and writhing, and shaking . . . they're just like animals!"

There was no response from Henry; he just sipped his drink, watched and grinned. Mrs. Ferris caught his expression and nudged him so hard, it caught him off balance a second. He turned his attention away from the dancers and with real determination, he shook his head disapprovingly.

Pat and Joe took their chairs and began to relax as Pat continued to watch the Ferrises. The conversation from the adjoining table drifted their way as they overheard two spinster-type women exchanging their appraisals of the rest of the guests. "Look at her . . . all dolled up. But did you ever see her home? I know they could afford to have someone come in to clean if she's too lazy to do it herself," one criticized.

"That's not all," the other chimed in; "did you ever take a good look at her kids? They all have runny noses. If she spent as much time on them as she does on her hairdos, well . . ."

"See these Christians, how they love one another?" Joe whispered in mock profoundness.

"There go the Ferrises to the punch bowl again," Pat informed.

Joe felt a gentle tap on his shoulder. He turned quickly.

"Hello."

"Jennie!" Joe gazed at her awkwardly for a moment, than stood. "Are you a guest? Do you want to sit down?" he stammered. *(What is* she *doing here?)*

"I saw you come in a while ago; but you seemed pretty tied up, so I waited until you had a free minute. You're looking well, Joe. The life must agree with you."

"Who are you with?" *(That's a dumb thing to ask . . . it's none of my business.)*

"I met some people here tonight . . . we're all friends of the Marshall family. I knew this was your parish . . . my mother told me. I was wondering if I'd see you here tonight."

"I always try to stop by the wedding receptions . . . it's kind of expected." There was an awkward silence until Pat excused himself to visit with Father John's group for a while.

"Can't you sit down for a while?" Joe asked.

Jennie took the chair Pat had vacated. "I guess you heard about my divorce?"

"My mother mentioned it. I was sorry to hear it. How are you and the kids getting on?"

"Better, now . . . but it was difficult at first. That's why we moved back here from Chicago. The children are better off this way. The last few years with Gary were unbearable, not only for me, but for them too. He lost one job after another and he'd go away for days, never hearing a word from him until his money ran out. Finally he just left and didn't come back. Next thing I knew, he was calling me from San Francisco to ask for a divorce. He met a girl there and decided he wanted out so he could be free to marry her. Anyway, that's past history now." She reached in her purse. "Let me show you a picture of my kids." *(She's still beautiful. Her looks haven't changed . . . hair's a little different, more makeup than she used to wear.)*

"Here they are," she pointed out. "That's Billy, he's nine . . . Chris, he's seven . . . and Kathy, she's five."

"They're beautiful." Joe studied the little faces, then returned the pictures.

"I'm proud of them, Joe. They're all I really care about . . . now. You know, Joe, I wanted to call you so often when I first got back, but then I began going to a priest in the parish nearby. I was confused, perhaps a little bitter, but he's helped me a lot."

"Good. I'm glad to hear that. If he's helping, you should continue with *his* counseling." *(Was that too obvious?)*

"I intend to . . ."

Again, awkward silence. *(What should I say? I know she must remember the times we shared together as much as I do . better stay away from that . . . too nostalgic!)*

"Maybe I'll have a chance to meet your children soon. I suppose they visit your mother often." He hastened to add, "Since Mom lives right next door, I'll probably run into them."

"That would be nice." She paused a moment, then stood to leave. "Well, Joe, it was nice seeing you again." She held out her hand.

"Good seeing you too, Jennie." He squeezed her hand gently. "And take care of that lovely family of yours . . ." he called after as she walked away. *(I was awfully professional with her . . . professional, but prudent.)* Joe remembered Marge Harris as he had seen her that very morning. *("It just happened, Father . . ." I handled this the right way. I won't let it just happen to me . . .)*

Joe decided he had committed himself to the social graces long enough. He was about to find Pat when an excited young man hurried towards him. "Father, someone on the parking lot needs a priest right away!"

Joe followed the young man out of the hall. The scene had created a slight commotion and a few guests tailed after them to find out what was the trouble.

"Over there, Father . . . in the car."

In the darkness, Joe saw a man's figure slumped over the steering wheel. Hurriedly, he leaned the man against the back of the seat, then loosened his tie and belt. "I saw Doctor Reardon in the hall. Get someone to page him," Joe said as he looked at the man's face closely. "Henry Ferris!"

"Is he gonna die? What's wrong with him?" Mrs. Ferris cried in almost inaudible words.

"Stay calm, Mrs. Ferris. We're getting help."

She began to rock back and forth with her hands resting on the dashboard. "He never looked like this before. Oh, my God!"

"Open your door . . . give him more air," Joe directed.

Pat jumped in the back seat of the car and leaned forward. "Can I help? I saw you run out of the hall . . . figured something was up."

"Move away, everybody . . . give the doctor room," Joe commanded as Doctor Reardon leaned over the patient, took his pulse, then lifted his eyelids. Mr. Ferris stirred slightly. "My bag's in that white Olds," the physician said to no one in particular, jerking his head in the direction of a "Ninety-Eight."

Pat jumped from the car and was back within seconds with the doctor's case.

"My God . . . what's happenin'? Henry . . . Oh, God . . ." Mrs. Ferris continued to rock back and forth, now pressing her hands to her cheeks with her eyes never leaving her husband's face.

The doctor unbuttoned Mr. Ferris' shirt to the waist to listen with his stethoscope. "Get those people away from the car, Father." His voice was unusually calm . . . not at all professional.

Pat took command and ordered the curious onlookers to return to the hall. When his audience disbanded, the doctor began slapping Henry's face vigorously.

"What are you doin'?" Mrs. Ferris screamed.

"I'm getting him to come to," the doctor explained, smiling. (*I don't get it . . . what's going on?*)

181

"Get her to calm down, will you?" the doctor asked Joe.

"What's wrong with him?" Joe was confused.

"Just take a good look at him . . . he's bombed out of his mind, that's all."

"He's what? What's wrong with my Henry? Why arn'cha tellin' me the truth? It's serious, izzn'it?" She cried out.

"She's not in too good of a shape either, from the sound of her," the doctor whispered to Joe, then directed his attention to Mrs. Ferris. "Your husband will be all right. Take him home and put him to bed." He turned back to Joe. "Let the old guy sleep it off. He'll need a doctor more tomorrow then he does tonight. That poor son of a gun is going to have a hangover out of this world."

"You're still not tellin' me what's wrong with Henry!"

"I told you, Mrs. Ferris, he's fine . . . just take him home."

"What kinda doctor are you? Arn'cha gonna give him a sub-scrip . . ., a perpsprip . . . a spercri . . . arn'cha gonna give him some *medicine?*" Her eyes were glazed and her cheeks, flushed, as she stared at the doctor.

"No, black coffee . . . two cups every half hour for the next hour will take care of it," Reardon said with a hearty laugh.

Joe stood upright away from Mrs. Ferris' view and began to laugh almost uncontrollably. He stopped long enough to thank Doctor Reardon, then called Pat to the car. "Here's my keys. Pull my car around to the lot, then you follow me while I drive them home. I can drive back with you."

Joe made certain the door was securely shut on Mrs. Ferris' side, then slid Henry away from the wheel to the middle of the seat. Joe reached in Henry's jacket pocket searching for the keys.

"Whaddaya doin' to Henry?" she slurred as the effects of the spiked punch worsened.

"Looking for the keys . . . where does he keep them?"

"I'll get 'em!" she answered protectively, then reached in the right pants pocket and retrieved the keys. She swayed a bit as she handed them to Joe.

"Thank you," Joe said, trying hard not to begin laughing all over again. He started the ignition, then waited for Pat.

Mrs. Ferris put her left arm around her husband and rested his head on her shoulder while she patted his cheek. "There now, Pun'kin, I'll take care of you." *(Pun'kin? . . . so Henry is "Pumpkin.")*

Henry opened his eyes momentarily, snuggled closer to his wife, then closed his eyes again. "I don't feel good, Boopsie," he said pathetically. *(Boopsie! . . . no! How could he pick a name like "Boopsie" for her? It's hard to imagine, but I guess they were young once. Somehow I just pictured her starting kindergarten in a grey print jersey dress, black oxfords and a tight permanent. Boopsie! . . . Boopsie, I hope you remember all this in the morning.)*

Pat sounded the horn to give Joe the cue to go on. By the time they pulled just a few blocks away, Joe's passengers were both fast asleep.

They didn't even stir as he parked the car in their drive. Joe went to the passenger's side and unlocked the door. "Mrs. Ferris, wake up . . . you're home."

"Yes; yes, so I am . . ." she said sternly, then poked Henry hard enough to bring him back to full consciousness. "C'mon, Henry. Get out," she ordered, "we're home."

Pat was already standing by the car. Joe threw the keys to him. "Find the house key and get the door, will you? I'll get them."

Pat opened the door and switched on the foyer light as Mrs. Ferris held on to her husband and with very deliberate steps, entered the house. A white miniature poodle came yapping away to meet them.

"Ah, there's my little Fifi. Come to Mama," she said in "baby talk," then let go of Henry's arm as he fell against the wall. She lifted the dog to her face and kissed it. "Fifi gotta go potty? Sure, 'cause Mama's been gone a long time . . . yes, her has."

Joe placed the keys on the drum table by the window. "Let's get out of here and let Pumpkin, Boopsie and Fifi go to bed," he laughed.

"Who?" Pat asked in a voice full of incredulity as he closed the door behind him.

183

The parking lot was beginning to empty when Joe and Pat returned.

"You going back to the hall?" Pat asked.

"No, the janitor's car is there already. He'll lock up when everybody leaves and start cleaning the place up before the Masses tomorrow."

Joe locked the garage and was turning away when he caught sight of Jennie leaving the parking lot as her car pulled into the light of the street lamp. Joe stood there and watched her until her car was out of view.

"You coming, Father?" Pat called. "What are you looking at?"

"An old friend," Joe answered as he walked to the rectory door.

CHAPTER 12

FOREVER AND EVER

(Sunday)

Joe gazed into the congregation as the lector began the first reading. The news had already spread that Joe was their new pastor. Certainly this provoked concern for their old administrator, Monsignor Flannagan. After all, he had served them well for the past twenty years. The conclusion was natural: a man they had come to love was no longer able to continue to meet their needs. But what were their needs? Baptizing their babies? Marrying their children? Visiting their sick? Anointing their dying? Listening to their problems? Absolving their sins?

And each week they put aside all other obligations to fulfill their duty as Christians, to worship their Lord, to tap the reservoir of infinite strength to help them through the rest of the week. And what man did they rely on to provide them with their spiritual food? Their parish priest! Yet, he too was a man like themselves, with the same frailties, weaknesses, frustrations and anxieties. What made him different from them? Why did they place so much trust in another human? What could he offer them? Joe suddenly realized that the words of inspiration he had outlined so conscientiously the night before didn't seem meaningful any longer, under these circumstances here at St. Monica's.

When the Gospel ended, he looked out upon his congregation, totally aware of their need and his own human inadequacy. He rejected all the thoughts he had prepared. Now, he had a different message. Silently he prayed to the Holy Spirit to help him find the right words. He paused for a moment, resting his hands on the sides of the pulpit; then in deep deliberate tones he began.

"Christ had two natures, human and divine. Jesus, our Savior and God, was first a man. He was born of a woman . . He had flesh and blood . . . He cried for his milk . . . He stumbled and fell . . . He grew up in a family and was tucked into bed at night by His mother. First, He was a boy, then He became a man. He was a man with a divine plan, a plan that needed His human body and mind as a victim, His human body as a priest. He had a plan to save all men. Christ was a priest first. It started at the moment of His conception. It continued to grow when He was laid as an infant in the manger at Bethlehem. He lay in the stable with all the dignity of His priesthood. Also as a small wrapped baby, He lay in the manger, the helpless sacrificial *victim* to be offered for all mankind.

"He was the eternal priest and the eternal victim . . . Jesus suffered long before Calvary. . . . He suffered when He gazed into the eyes of the poor, the sick, the oppressed . . . He suffered with mankind in every human tragedy . . . He suffered in His humanity more than any other human. Yet, He shared the joys of men too . . . He celebrated with them at the wedding feast of Cana . . . at the religious festivals in Jerusalem. Jesus was a man among men, a man who was also divine. . . . His divinity was hidden in human flesh . . . thousands of people who saw Him and listened to Him could never penetrate His human disguise . . . they saw only Jesus the man. To the few chosen, He was more . . . He was the Messiah, the Christ, the Son of God!

"Did Christ's priesthood finish at Calvary? Did His concern for man stop that Good Friday? Was that the end of Jesus, the eternal victim, the eternal priest? No! His priesthood is eternal, for He breathed on His Apostles and said, 'Receive the Holy Spirit; if you forgive men's sins, they are forgiven . . . go to all nations and baptize them.' Christ still walks the earth . . . He still looks into the eyes of the poor, the sick, the oppressed . . . He still celebrates with men at weddings, parties and festivals.

"He still enters the homes and hearts of all men in all parts of the world. He still dines with the rich and the poor, for He is still clothed in human flesh. He is still a man among men in the person of a priest. He is present at every baptism . . . He forgives sins every time a priestly hand is raised in absolution . . . He continues His work in the disguise of the human priests who participate daily in His eternal priesthood."

Joe paused for a few moments, again searching.

"Christ has two natures — the human and divine," he repeated, "as does the priesthood itself. For He takes men's humanity and uses it to bring His people to the divine. All of us who are ordained share in the eternal priesthood of Christ. Today, I want to tell you about one of His priests, Monsignor Flannagan. Although the body of Monsignor Flannagan has surrendered to a serious illness which prohibits him from remaining at St. Monica's as your pastor, his work is continued through Christ's working in the other priests who are sent here to serve you. The priesthood of Christ continues whether in the person of the Pope, Bishop Condry, Father Benetti, or me. Tolerate our weaknesses . . . we are human. And pray that we always are mindful of our calling, to continue the work of Christ.

"Now as you leave Mass and speak of Monsignor Flannagan, recalling how much he has done for you and St. Monica's, praise him for his work, pay him the compliments which he deserves. But pay him the compliment he would be most proud of: remember to say, 'Monsignor Flannagan is a *good* priest!' "

Since Pat volunteered to take care of the rectory, Joe decided to take advantage of a beautiful Sunday. After the last Mass, he went to his room and changed into a pair of khaki pants and a sport shirt. He had a promise to keep and Timmy Newman never forgot a promise. Today was a beautiful day to try out his nephew's new football . . . besides, he needed the exercise.

Joe decided to take the "long way" to his brother's home and drive through the park. The quiet of the surroundings and fresh air tempted Joe to relax alone for a while. He parked the car off the main drive and looked over the lake where benches were scattered here and there *(Why not? . . . I got plenty of time.)* Slowly he walked down the hill to the one of the benches that sat just a few feet from the water. He stretched out his legs and spread his arms on the backrest of the bench, then tilted his head back. *(Feel that warm breeze ... beautiful!)* The only sound that broke the quiet was the rustling of the dry leaves and the chirping of the birds. *(Solitude can sometimes be a luxury ... I could get lost here for hours ... no phones, no messages, no clocks, nothing but quiet and sunshine.)* He was almost ready to doze when a faint sound brought him back: it sounded like a ball game broadcast. Joe looked around. A man was walking down the hill carrying a transistor radio in one hand and a small cooler in the other. He made his way straight to Joe's bench.

"Mind if I sit down, fella?" he said, crooking his mouth to keep his cigar in place.

Joe nodded. "What's the score?"

"Two nothin' ... we're losin'!"

Joe's new companion became engrossed in the game. He leaned toward the radio which he had placed on the bench between them and listened intently as he reached in his cooler and pulled out a can of beer. "Want one?"

"No, thanks." *(Friendly guy.)*

"Like that fresh air, don't ya, fella?" He took a sip of beer. "Me too. A man has to get away once in a while."

Joe looked at him more closely; he looked as if he may have been in his late forties, rather stout and not much hair left. He removed his cigar from his mouth only long enough to flick away the ashes.

"Do you come here often?" Joe asked.

"Every Sunday ... come here to get away from all the noise at home. The old lady has a fit too. She says, 'Charlie, how come you never want to spend Sunday afternoons takin' a ride with me?' I say, 'The oldest kid knows how to drive; have him take you.' She gets mad and says I don't want to spend my time with her and the kids. Can you beat that? I work like a son of a gun all week long ... work damn hard, too. I have to listen to all that bull at the plant ... everybody's got troubles. You know, I got a teen-age girl who won't talk to me 'cause I won't give her money to buy hot pants. I tell her, 'Ain't no kid of mine gonna run around at thirteen in hot pants!' Ain't that right?" He nudged Joe. Joe nodded. "Then she says she'll use her baby-sittin' money to buy them with . . . I tell her I don't care where the money comes from, 'cause ain't no kid of mine gonna run around in hot pants! Man, kids today are somethin' else! You got kids?"

Joe shook his head negatively and was about to elaborate when his friend interrupted him again. "But you know, kids are great. I love my kids. Hell, if I didn't love them, I wouldn't work so damn hard . . . eight to five, five days a week. Punch that time clock and make that dough . . . keep the family happy. The wife, she thinks I enjoy myself when I leave for work every day. She says, 'At least you get to get out of the house . . . you get to talk to people.' Ain't that a damn shame? She's bellyachin' about not talkin' to people and I can't even call home that the phone ain't busy. What the hell does she do on that phone? . . . Ain't usin' sign language, right?"

Joe nodded.

The man stopped to take a huge gulp of beer. "Ah, that's good. Have me a can or two every night when I come home from work. It's hot in that plant . . . and I work hard. I like to relax when I get home. You know, kick off my shoes, open a can of cold beer, read the newspaper, have supper with the family, then watch the evenin' news. Man, I can't understand why they take them westerns off the air, can you?" Joe shrugged. "A man likes a little *adult* entertainment, right?" Joe nodded. "Work hard all day, need to relax at night, ain't that right?" Joe nodded again. "Yep, I come here every Sunday though. I tell the wife, 'Look, I ain't stoppin' you from goin' to them bingos or shows once in a while, so don't get on me about my Sunday afternoons.' Hell, I ain't gone but a few hours, get home in time for supper, and she says, 'But you don't love me, or you'd want to spend your day off with me.' Ain't that nuts? You ever get that stuff from your ol' lady?"

"As a matter of fact, I'm . . ."

"That lake's beautiful, ain't it?" The man didn't let Joe finish. "Only one thing bad about it . . . when I get ready to go after I finish my beer, I always think about goin' back to the plant Monday mornin' and all the work I got all week long. Know what I mean?" Joe nodded. "But you know, I been there twenty years . . . in line for a supervisor's job, now. It's a good raise, but a

189

lotta responsibility. I gotta stay on my toes . . . make sure all the appliances come out tip-top shape . . . I'm in waffle irons. I'll kinda be like an inspector. Know what I mean?" Joe agreed with a nod. "Yes sir, a man's entitled to a day of rest . . . says so in the Bible, don't it?"

Joe was about to answer when Charlie raised his hand and motioned for Joe to shut up. He didn't want to miss a crucial play in the game. Joe sat back until the play was completed.

"Damn it! I figured that would happen! They're gonna lose the game now for sure . . . might as well sit back and relax." He switched off the radio. "Sure you don't want a beer, fella?"

Joe nodded by mistake, saying quickly, "I mean, no . . . no, thanks." Charlie didn't seem to hear Joe as he pulled the tab on his second can of beer, then sat back and stretched out. "This is the life. Hey, fella, what do you do for a living?"

"I'm a priest," Joe answered simply.

"No kidding! You're a priest? I'll be damned! Then I guess you don't know what I been talkin' about. What I mean is . . . like Sunday is your big work day . . . but what do you guys have to do *the rest of the week?*"

ALSO BY FATHER ROBERTS:

PRAY IT AGAIN, SAM! . . . combines just the right amount of wit, instruction and inspiration to create a truly delightful reading experience. It appeals to all ages and will be treasured by anyone seeking spiritual growth. Father explains various ways to pray with emphasis on the PRAYER OF LISTENING. He refers to the Old Testament and the book of Samuel. Samuel didn't recognize when the Lord was speaking to him . . . do you?

(paperback . . . $3.95)   PAX TAPES PUBLISHERS

MARY, THE PERFECT PRAYER PARTNER . . . is a beautiful book that offers a unique picture of Mary's role in the church, her role as a model for all Christians, and her special role as the 'perfect prayer partner.' In Part II of this book, Father Roberts invites you to follow with him the Scriptural events of each of the fifteen mysteries of the rosary as he asks the questions:

How did it feel, Mary?
How did it feel, Jesus?
How did it feel, early Christians?

(paperback . . . $3.95)   PAX TAPES PUBLISHERS

OTHER BOOKS BY FATHER ROBERTS:

PLAYBOY TO PRIEST . . . In his autobiography, Father Roberts tells of his unique journey to the priesthood.

YOU BETTER BELIEVE IT . . . This popular catechism offers answers to youth in their own language, about God, the Church, and about themselves.

AUDIO AND VIDEO CASSETTES ALSO AVAILABLE:

Father Roberts teaches a complete course on the beliefs and practices of the Catholic Church in an easy-to-understand language. He answers many of the questions mostly asked of Catholics about their faith. Other topics are also available.

For more information, and to order Father's books, write to:
PAX TAPES INC.
P.O. Box 1059
Florissant, Missouri 63031